John Lowe

The Yew-Trees of Great Britain and Ireland

John Lowe

The Yew-Trees of Great Britain and Ireland

ISBN/EAN: 9783337322458

Printed in Europe, USA, Canada, Australia, Japan

Cover: Foto ©Andreas Hilbeck / pixelio.de

More available books at **www.hansebooks.com**

THE YEW-TREES

OF GREAT BRITAIN

AND IRELAND

BY

JOHN LOWE, M.D. Ed.

HONORARY PHYSICIAN TO HIS ROYAL HIGHNESS
THE PRINCE OF WALES; FELLOW OF THE
LINNÆAN SOCIETY; FELLOW OF THE
BOTANICAL SOCIETY OF EDINBURGH
ETC. ETC.

London

MACMILLAN AND CO., Limited

NEW YORK: THE MACMILLAN COMPANY

1897

All rights reserved

TO MY WIFE

'What of the bow?
    The bow was made in England;
Of true wood, of yew wood,
    The wood of English bows;
        So men who are free
        Love the old yew-tree,
And the land where the yew-tree grows.'

A. CONAN DOYLE.

PREFACE

SOME years ago I commenced an inquiry into certain points bearing on peculiarities in the rate of growth, and having relation to the age, of yew-trees. Since then the investigation has been continued and extended. A large amount of material has thus been accumulated, which, it is thought, may be of future as well as present interest, and which should not, therefore, be allowed to die. This record of the most notable trees in Great Britain and Ireland is sent forth with the addition of much interesting matter, kindred to the subject, which has been found scattered in many publications, and is now collated with, I trust, due acknowledgment of all the sources of information. The account of Scottish yews has been largely taken from Mr. Hutchison's paper.[1] Of the greater number of English trees comparatively few are at all known, and even of these no collected notice

[1] 'Old and Remarkable Yew-trees in Scotland.'

has been printed. I would offer my best thanks to the very numerous correspondents, and especially to the large body of clergy, who have so kindly given me data and measurements of notable trees. To Mr. W. Robinson I am under great obligations for much valuable assistance and advice, and to Mr. F. W. Burbidge for most of the information about Irish trees.

CONTENTS

	PAGE
INTRODUCTION	1

CHAPTER I

Taxus baccata, L.—Varieties—Etymology of Yew—Epithets 19

CHAPTER II

Geographical distribution—Indigenous—Geological remains—Sparse distribution in England—Reasons for this. 26

CHAPTER III

Age of yew-trees—Considered slow-growing—Mode of estimating age—Traditional accounts—Age of contiguous buildings—De Candolle's method of calculating age—Rings of growth—In young trees correct—In old, erroneous—Rejuvenescence—Increase by welding of young shoots—Variable growth 35

CHAPTER IV

Rate of growth—Point of measurement—Sir R. Christison's view—Objections—Instances—Measurements of trees of known age—Increase at fixed points and at stated periods—Examples—Dr. Christison's and Dr. Beddoe's measurements—Mr. Bowman's method—Trephine—Objections—Traditional accounts—Fallacies—Rate of growth in old trees—Periods of rest and growth   47

CHAPTER V

Causes of variation in growth—Retardation and acceleration — Pollarding — its meaning — Frequency — Causes—Results—Rings of wood—Hollow trunks becoming solid   .   .   .   66

CHAPTER VI

Notable trees and their measurements—in England and Wales—in Scotland and in Ireland—All trees of 10 feet in girth and upwards—Trees of 30 feet in girth and upwards, in England and Wales   81

CHAPTER VII

Why planted in churchyards—Druidical, Roman, and Christian customs—Early English writers—Funeral customs—Symbolism—Shelter of buildings—For providing bow wood — Hansard's objections — Planted in churchyards in Germany and Normandy   96

CHAPTER VIII

Characters of yew wood—Uses—Manufacture--Value —'Saint's Yew   107

CHAPTER IX

Bows—Ancient use—Long-bow—Battle of Hastings—Its value in English wars—English supremacy—Various Statutes — Forest laws — Edward II.—Edward III.—Edward IV.—French archers—Statute of Henry VIII.—Elizabeth—'Act of Bowyers'—Prices—Importation of foreign bows—Act of Philip and Mary—Companies of Archers—Commission of Charles I.—Bow-making—Cross-bows made of yew —Its inferiority to the long-bow . .   111

CHAPTER X

Poisonous properties of the yew—Classical notices—Wood—Leaves—Fruit poisonous—Dangerous statements to the contrary—Effects on man—Taxin in male and female plants—Medicinal use—Valuable as a cardiac tonic—Poisonous effects on animals .   136

CHAPTER XI

Poetical allusions, etc., to the yew in ancient and modern times 154

CHAPTER XII

Notes, historical, etc., on some of the more remarkable trees 180

BIBLIOGRAPHY 261

INDEX 265

LIST OF ILLUSTRATIONS

FULL-PAGE ILLUSTRATIONS

1. The Patterdale Yew		*Frontispiece*
2. The Four Evangelists and Twelve Apostles, Cleve Prior	*facing page*	7
3. Clipped Yews at Levens Hall	,,	11
4. Clipped Yew Avenue, Painswick	,,	15
5. Yew Avenue, Royal Botanical Gardens, Glasnevin, Dublin	,,	18
6. Yew-tree in Yewdale, Coniston	,,	23
7. ,, at Cherkley Court	,,	28
8. ,, Albury Park, Surrey	,,	32
9. ,, Crowhurst, Sussex	,,	38
10. Sunshine and Shade, Yew Terrace, Castle Ward, Downpatrick	,,	48
11. 'The Queen,' Cherkley Court	,,	63
12. Yew-trees in Borrodale	,,	68
13. The Patterdale Yew	,,	83
14. Yew-trees in Druids' Grove, Norbury Park	,,	97
15. Yew at Warblington	,,	100
16. Norman Archers	,,	112
17. Yew Avenue near Penrhyn Castle	,,	137
18. Yew at Brockenhurst	,,	193
19. Yew in Leeds Churchyard, Kent	,,	227
20. The Patterdale Yew	,,	242

21. Yew-tree at Tisbury	*facing page* 251
22. Yew-tree at Trentham (A)	,, 253
23. Yew in Warblington Churchyard	,, 256

ILLUSTRATIONS IN TEXT

1. Under Yew-trees: Gravetye Manor, Sussex	*page* 17
2. Yew at Fountain's Abbey	39
3. Yew affected by Galls	71
4. Sectional View of Yew-tree in Bredhurst Churchyard, Kent	78
5. Sectional View of Yew-tree in Norbury Park	79
6. ,, Yew-trees at Tintern	79
7. English 'Double-armed Man,' 1625	126
8. Yew-tree in Wilmington Churchyard	135
9. Yew-tree at Killyleigh Castle, Co. Down	153
10. ,, South Hayling	179
11. Sectional View of Yew at Ashtead, Surrey	185
12. Yew at Boughton-under-Blean	189
13. Harlington Yew, 1729	220
14. Mamhilad Yew	233
15. Yew at Trentham (B)	253
16. ,, ,, (C)	254

INTRODUCTION

THERE is no English tree which has gathered round itself so much of historic, poetic, and legendary lore as the Yew; none is so closely associated, directly or indirectly, with events, persons, and buildings, which are famous in our national history. In early and mediæval times it was a source of our country's greatness and supremacy, by supplying the bows and arrows with which our great victories were won; but in spite of this, it has never attained that love and veneration in the popular mind, so lavishly bestowed on its rival, the oak, which has played such a conspicuous part in the successes of later days.

While men look upon the yew in wonder at its hoary age and vast antiquity, there is in their minds none of the cheery, reverential feeling inspired by the 'brave old oak,' but rather a sense of awe, produced by the sombre and gloomy shade of its foliage, and the deathly character it bears, in all its relations.

The literature which treats of it, even from the earliest times, bears an impression of sadness, and most of the poetic allusions to it have more or less of the same character. Du Hamel du Monceau is one of the few writers who takes a higher view of its teaching :—

'Sa forme conique et l'épaisseur de son feuillage, toujours verd, mais sombre, insensible aux changements des saisons et des années lui donnent un caractère de gravité qui dispose l'esprit au recueillement qu'exigent l'étude et la méditation, inspire des grandes idées, et rappelle de touchants souvenirs.'

Notwithstanding the gloom which seems to surround the yew, it is a tree of which Englishmen may well be proud, as having served, equally with the oak, to place England in her present exalted position.

Creçy, Poictiers, Agincourt, and many other hard-fought fields, tell of the one; the defeat of the Spanish Armada, the battles of the Nile and Trafalgar, of the other.

Then again, both trees have had a quasi-sacred character; the oak with its mistletoe having played an important part in Druidical mysteries, and being still regarded as emblematic of rugged strength and endurance, while the yew, from its perpetual verdure, the durability of its wood, and its power of rejuvenescence, has from the earliest times been used in funeral rites, and has been held to symbolise the resurrection, and the immortality of the soul.

Introduction

Putting aside what may be considered merely sentimental views concerning the yew, it has an intrinsic value which has not in modern times received the recognition it deserves. In earlier days there were special enactments for the culture and protection of the yew. From the time of Edward IV. to a somewhat late period in the reign of Elizabeth, these Acts continued in force, renewed by each successive sovereign, and it was not until the latter reign, when fire-arms came into more general use, that less consideration was paid to the long-bow. The last Statute issued with regard to the use of bows is the 13th Elizabeth (cap. xiv.), which orders that bow-staves shall be imported into England from the Hanse towns and other places. The hard, close-grained, tough and durable nature of the wood fit it for many useful purposes. It is not unlikely that its comparative scarceness is the sole reason for its disuse. Were it more largely planted, in districts where other trees cannot succeed, it would, in the space of sixty or seventy years, yield a supply of material valuable for many purposes for which other foreign and costly woods are now employed, and thus would add considerably to the internal resources of the country. Its varied uses are treated of subsequently. There is another point on which this tree has not received due appreciation, at any rate in recent times, viz., its value in landscape and ornamental gardening. If planted judiciously, and allowed free scope for its growth, it challenges all other evergreen trees for gracefulness of form. A tree of two hundred to two hundred and fifty years old, standing alone and well-grown, is one of the most beautiful of British trees. But it is peculiarly sensitive to overcrowding, and if light and air be excluded by the pressure of other trees, its lower branches soon die off, and the perfectness of its form is marred.

When planted skilfully and arranged in contrast with other trees, it is capable of producing charming effects.

Mr. W. Robinson says:[1] 'When, after a very hard winter, we see the evergreen trees of the garden in mourning, and perhaps many a stem dead, as happens to Laurels, Laurustinuses, and often even the Bay, it is a good time to consider the hardiness and other good qualities of our British evergreens, and the many forms raised from them. If we are fortunate enough to have old Yew-trees near us, we do not find that a hard winter makes any difference to them, even winters that sear the evergreen Oak. We have collected within the past two hundred years evergreen trees from all parts of the northern world, but it is doubtful if any of them are better than the common Yew, which, when old, is often picturesque, and which

[1] *The Wild Garden*, p. 268.

lives green for a thousand years.' Gilpin, in 1791, says:[1] 'I profess myself (contrary, I suppose, to the general opinion) a great admirer of its form and foliage. The Yew is, of all other trees, the most tonsile. Hence all the indignities it suffers. We everywhere see it cut and metamorphosed into such a variety of deformities, that we are hardly brought to conceive it has a natural shape, or the power which other trees have of hanging carelessly and negligently.

'Yet it has this power in a very eminent degree; and in a state of nature, except in exposed situations, is perhaps one of the most beautiful evergreens we have. Indeed I know not whether, all things considered, it is not superior to the cedar of Lebanon itself.'

In ornamental gardening it was employed as early as the Tudor times to form hedges, which were 'pleached' and clipped into the forms of grotesque beasts, birds, cones, pyramids, or other fantastic shapes. During the seventeenth century the taste for this kind of art increased, and in the time of William and Mary had reached its highest point.

Lord Bacon had in the previous century condemned the practice. 'I for my part,' he says,[2] 'do not like images cut out in juniper and other garden stuff; they be for children.'

Evelyn claims 'without vainitie' the credit of

[1] *Remarks on Forest Scenery.*   [2] *Essays.*

being the first who brought the Yew 'into fashion, as well for a defence as for a succedaneum to cypress, whether in hedges or pyramids, conic spires, bowls, or what other shapes. . . . I do again name the yew, for hedges, preferable for beauty and a stiff defence, to any plant I have ever seen.'

While perhaps not admiring these birds and beasts, we must, I think, in a measure agree with Loudon, that many old-fashioned gardens have suffered in losing the quaint forms of cropped yews, which added a certain charm to them.

It was mainly due to the ridicule thrown upon the practice by Addison and Pope that it fell into disuse. Pope derides the fashion for cutting trees into figures.

'An eminent town gardener,' he says, 'has arrived at such perfection, that he cuts family pieces of men, women, or children in trees.'

'Adam and Eve in Yew, Adam a little shattered by the fall of the tree of knowledge in the great storm; Eve and the serpent very flourishing. St. George in box, his arm scarce long enough, but will be in a condition to stick the dragon by next April; a green dragon of the same with a tail of ground-ivy for the present. (*N.B.*—These two not to be sold separately.) Divers eminent modern poets in bays, somewhat blighted, to be disposed of a pennyworth. A quickset hog, shot up into

THE FOUR EVANGELISTS AND TWELVE APOSTLES, CLEVE PRIOR.

From a picture by Mr. E. R. Taylor, *Edgbaston.*

a porcupine, by its being forgot a week in rainy weather.'

The Four Evangelists and Twelve Apostles at Cleve Prior are finely depicted by Mr. E. R. Taylor in a painting in the Exhibition of the Royal Academy in the year 1896.

Bradley says in 1717:[1] 'I have seen great varieties of figures, and very well represented, of men, beasts, birds, ships, and the like; but the most common shapes which have been given to the yew by gardeners are either cones or pyramids.' On account of the smallness of its leaves, he thinks the yew best adapted for clipping into the forms of animals; 'the holly and other broad-leaved evergreens are not fit for being cut into any nicer figures than pyramids, balls, or a straight stem with a top like the cap of a mushroom.'

Collinson notes that the gardens about London in 1712 were remarkable for fine cut greens and clipped yews, in the shape of birds, dogs, men, ships, etc. The most remarkable instance still exists at Packwood, Warwickshire, where the Sermon on the Mount is literally represented in clipped yew.

Very many yew hedges and clipped trees were swept away in the middle of the eighteenth century by a man named Brown, who was gardener at Hampton Court. He dealt ruthlessly with all

[1] *New Improvements*, p. 72.

clipped hedges and topiary work, but there appears to have been a natural rebound in the public mind with regard to yew hedges after the attacks of Addison and Pope, and the wholesale manner they were swept away to make room for Brown's new style of landscape-gardening. Thus we find Knight expressing his dissatisfaction with the modern idea, and longing for a return to the former state of things :—

> 'Tired with the extensive scene, so dull and bare,
> To Heaven devoutly I've address'd my prayer;
> Again the moss-grown terraces to raise,
> And spread the labyrinth's perplexing maze;
> Replace in even lines the ductile yew,
> And plant again the ancient avenue.'[1]

Nor is it to be wondered at that the sheltered walks which let in the sun but kept out the wind, affording such delightful promenades, should be greatly missed in spring and autumn, as the cold blasts blew without opposition through the now-exposed and shelterless garden.

Mr. Robinson, in his delightfully suggestive book, *The Wild Garden*, says that he uses them as a shelter for orchards, planting them some distance apart, with flowering plants and shrubs between, and clematis or bindweed to climb over them. Some lovely effects would be produced in this way, but much care would be needed that

[1] R. P. Knight, 2nd ed., 1795.

the creepers be not allowed to grow too thickly, as there would be danger of the trees being killed.

A good many clipped hedges and old avenues, fortunately, escaped destruction, though probably not very many are of great age. The Hon. Miss Amherst in her charming book[1] mentions that an 'interesting garden of the Tudor date is at the Palace, Hadham, in Hertfordshire, which for many hundred years belonged to the Bishops of London. It was also the dwelling-place of Katherine, widow of Henry v., after her marriage with Owen Tudor, and it was here that Edmund, father of Henry vii., was born. The garden at the present day is surrounded on two sides by a wall, while the other side is protected by a high yew hedge, three yards thick.' It is somewhat doubtful if the hedges ascribed to this period date so far back as to Tudor times. I do not know of there being any of so great age. That at Henbury, near Bristol, in Mr. Sampson's garden, is pretty certainly two hundred years old, and I know not any of much greater age, except that at Milford, County Mayo. One of the trees in the hedge at Henbury has a girth of 6 feet 6 inches at the ground and 9 feet at 3 feet above that point. About one hundred years ago the hedge was cut down to its present height of 16 feet. This is shown by the old dead trunks being visible in the

[1] *History of Gardening in England*, p. 83.

centre, surrounded in some instances by a ring of secondary growth, also dead, outside which is a third ring of living wood. Two trees, one at the end of each hedge, and probably planted at the same time, have been left untrimmed for a long period. One of them is 12 feet in girth.

The yew hedges at Bishopsbourne, near Canterbury, says the Rev. Mr. Hirst, 'were planted by Richard Hooker about 1595, the year he came to Bishopsbourne; he could not have walked under their shade, as tradition asserts, as he was only there five years, having died in 1600. They are now about 14 feet high and 10 feet thick.'

'At Rockingham there remains a great terraced mound of earth, covered with turf and a few trees, raised against a part of the high wall which surrounds the garden, and behind which the keep formerly stood. From the top of this the eye ranges across the garden with quaintly cut yew-trees, over a magnificent view of the open country beyond.'

'The quaintly-rounded hedges and the hedges and trees at Erbistock are examples of the cut yews of this date. That of Bilton, in Warwickshire, with its fine holly and yew hedges, was begun in 1623.'[1]

Some fine examples of 'topiary' are shown in an engraving, in *History of Gardening in England*,

---

[1] *History of Gardening in England*, pp. 78, 120, 128.

CLIPPED YEWS AT LEVENS HALL.

of the garden at Heslington, near York, which was laid out by Beaumont before 1687. The clipped yews would therefore date from this rather than from the Tudor period, 1560, when the house was built. The gardens at Hampton Court were laid out by the same person. The clipped yews at Levens, Westmoreland, are old and remarkable examples of this kind of work, the British Lion, Queen Elizabeth and ladies, the Judge's Wig, etc., being formed early in the eighteenth century.[1] At Albury there is a hedge 10 feet high and a quarter of a mile long, said to have been designed by Evelyn for the Earl of Arundel. At Bedfont, Middlesex, there are two large peacocks cut in yew, with the date 1708.[2] In Ireland there are some good hedges, as at Headfort, near Kells. At Milford, Co. Mayo, in the garden of Mr. Ormesby-Millen, there is one of great age, some of the trees being from 10 to 13 feet in girth, with the branches much welded together.'

The old yew-tree at Harlington, Middlesex, was clipped in 1729 into a series of circles, and must have been about 50 feet high. In 1780 or 1790 it ceased to be clipped, and was allowed to assume its natural form. It is now one of the finest trees

---

[1] *Gardener's Chronicle*, 1880.

[2] 'The local tradition is that they represent satirically two sisters who lived at Bedfont, and who were so very naughty that they both refused the hand of some local magnate, who thus immortalised their being "as proud as peacocks."'—Walford, *Greater London*, vol. i. p. 195.

in existence.[1] The yew-trees on the terrace at Haddon Hall were formerly clipped, but are now growing naturally into great trees.

Fine yew hedges are to be seen at Barncleuth, Haddingtonshire, and at Montacute, and there are also good examples at Rockingham, Brickwall, Northiam, Sussex; at Hutton John, near Penrith; at Wrest, Bedfordshire, a yew hedge twenty feet high surrounds the fish-pond.[2]

'At Melbourne, Derbyshire, and at Holme Lacy, Hereford, where they are magnificent and of extraordinary height and thickness.'[3] At Ashridge 'the wall enclosing a corner of the garden is part of the cloister, and near it there is also a third yew hedge enclosing another small piece of garden. Those at Arley, Cheshire, and at Penshurst, are said to be only twenty-five years old.'

At Helmarton Lodge, Calne, there are two hedges, $9\frac{1}{2}$ feet thick and about 60 yards in length. They are between forty-five and fifty years old.

The yew hedges at Coryton Park, Devon, date probably from 1756.

A charming effect is that produced at Aldby Park, near York. The lawn, on the river-front of the house, is bordered by clipped yew hedges, 15 feet in thickness, with marble statues in front; the hedges are backed by fine yew-trees, about 180 years old,

---

[1] *The Formal Garden.*   [2] *History of Gardening in England,* p. 26.
[3] Morris, *County Seats of Great Britain,* vol. i.

mixed with spruce and Scotch firs.¹ In the middle distance is a well-wooded country, and beyond are the Yorkshire wolds, looking blue in the distance. The whole makes a most striking and lovely picture. In the garden is another picturesque effect. The old Danish encampment, a high mound, surrounded by a dry moat, is covered with yew-trees, Scotch firs, and large box-trees, some of the firs having their red trunks partly covered with ivy. The general effect of colour with the foreground of flowers in the moat is very striking.

A yew hedge makes a fine background for the flower border, setting off the colours delightfully. Hollyhocks, dahlias, helianthuses, and asters are well shown up by the darker foliage of the yew.

In *Sir George Tressady*, Mrs. Humphry Ward has a beautiful imaginative passage describing a scene, made up of old ruins, clipped yew hedges, and masses of flowers, artistically 'mixed,' however, as to their blooming season. 'Amid the ruins of a cloister that had once formed part of the dissolved Cisterian priory, on whose confiscated lands Castle Luton had arisen, a rich medley of flowers were in full and perfect bloom. Irises in a very ravishing shade of purple, lilac and gold carpets, or daffodils and narcissus, covered the ground,

---

¹ The trees which form the hedge cannot be nearly as old as this, none of them having so much as a foot of diameter.

and ran into each corner and cranny of the old wall. Yellow banksia and white clematis climbed the crumbling shafts, or made new tracery for the empty windows, and where the ruins ended, yew hedges, adorned at top with a whole procession of birds and beasts, began. The flowery space thus enclosed was broken in the centre by an old fountain; and as one sat on a stone seat beside it, one looked through an archway, cut through the darkness of the yews, to the blue river and the hills.'

The rock-garden is never so well displayed as with a background formed by a yew hedge, which affords it a very efficient protection from cold winds or sun. It also makes a good shelter to a promenade in cold weather. The 'Green Gallery' at Melbourne is an arched avenue of densely interlaced boughs, probably resulting from a cropped hedge being afterwards allowed to grow naturally. It affords a deep shade. It is not especially beautiful or of great age, and must be very gloomy.

There is a very fine hedge in the garden of the Hon. Canon Bouverie at Pewsey, Wilts, the age of which is uncertain, but it is supposed to be three hundred years. 'It is 171 feet in length, 12 feet 9 inches high, and 7 feet wide. At each end there is a clump 18 feet high.'

Fine avenues of yew-trees are found at Roseneath, and at Cleish Castle, Kinross; at Llandagri,

CLIPPED YEW AVENUE, PAINSWICK.

North Wales; and at Painswick. These last, which number ninety-nine, are cropped.

In Brenchley Churchyard, Kent, there is an avenue of ten beautiful trees, which are kept carefully trimmed. There is also an avenue of yews at Candover, near Alresford, extending for nearly half a mile; the trees are planted along the road through Lord Ashburton's property, about 50 on either side; they are from 20 to 30 feet high; a good deal broken. They vary from 8 to 12 feet in girth, the latter having much young spray around the trunk. There is no record of the date when they were planted.

'The yew-trees of Overton-on-Dee, near Ellesmere, twenty-two in number, are many of them 10 feet in circumference, whilst one is close on 16 feet.'

At Aberglasney, Carnarvon, there is a remarkable avenue on the property of Lloyd Phillips, Esq. The branches on one side of a row of trees have been trained over and the ends planted so as to form a close alley. It probably dates from Jacobæan times.[1]

A striking example of good effects produced by the mixture of yews and forest trees is seen in the Clieveden Woods above Maidenhead, where there are some lovely combinations and contrasts of colour produced by groups of yew-trees, mixed

---

[1] *Gardener's Chronicle*, December 26, 1892.

with beech, sycamores, willows, etc., the whole surmounted by Scotch firs, with their red stems gleaming in the sunshine. This kind of effect is seen to greatest advantage on a hill-side. The Clieveden trees are with one exception not of any great age. On the upper and lower parts of the hill they are well-grown and vigorous, but those growing midway are much paler in colour and of various shades of yellow. This is evidently due to some peculiarity in the soil, which renders them unhealthy, as numbers are already dead.[1] These, when covered by a profuse growth of clematis, in flower, and backed by darker and more healthy yews, afford a picture of surprising beauty.

In Ireland there are some fine yew avenues where these trees appear to grow with great luxuriance and rapidity. At Glencormac, Co. Wicklow, in the grounds of R. S. Langworth-Damer, Esq., there is an avenue of ten trees having a girth of 10 feet and upwards.

At Clonfert, in King's County, there is another 284 yards in length, the trees of which have a girth of 6 to 8 feet.

There is an avenue of eleven very old trees on the property of Mrs. Jameson, Glencormack, near Bray. There are others at Mount Wilson, Eden-

---

[1] Some of these may have been killed by the clematis, but the number of dead trees on which there is no climber points to there being something deleterious in the soil.

Introduction

derry; at Gormanstown, near Balbriggan; at Longhern, Oldcastle, Co. Meath; and at Dunganstown Church, Co. Wicklow, there is 'a double row with splendid clear stems and grand heads.'

The yew-tree colonnade, at Dunganstown, Co. Wicklow (then the seat of William Hoey, Esq.) is thus mentioned by Hayes: 'I had the pleasure of finding an admired line of *yew-trees* in full vigour, as remarkable for their *form* as the chestnuts had been for their *size*. This consists of about thirty trees, most of them 6 feet round, perfectly straight and smooth in the stem as a young ash-

UNDER YEW-TREES: GRAVETYE MANOR, SUSSEX.
From photograph by Sir Henry Thompson, *kindly sent by* Mr. W. Robinson.

tree for about 7 feet 6 inches from the ground, where they begin to throw out branches, and thence continue a rich close mass of green foliage for full 25 feet above their clear stems, resembling a considerable superstructure raised over a regular colonnade. Had such a growth of *yew* been common in this kingdom in the days of archery, we should not have wanted Acts of Parliament requiring the importation of *yew bow*-staves from *Spain*.'

There are other avenues at Rossanagh, near Ashford; at Hurdlestone, Co. Clare; at Kilteevon, Roscommon; and at Glasnevin, a plate of the latter being given here.

YEW AVENUE, ROYAL BOTANICAL GARDEN, GLASNEVIN, DUBLIN
(ADDISON'S WALK).

From a photograph by Mr. D. Hemphill, M.D.

CHAPTER I

Taxus baccata, L.—Varieties—Etymology of Yew—Epithets.

Taxus baccata, Linn., the Common Yew, belongs to the genus *Taxus*, the type of the natural order *Taxaceæ*, of which the species are evergreen trees of low stature. The trunk rises usually from 5 to 10 feet from the ground, in rare instances reaching 15 to 20 feet, and then sending out numerous spreading branches which form a dense head of foliage, 30 to 50 feet in height, and 50 to 70 feet in diameter. The tallest yew in England is that at Harlington, near Hounslow, which, after being cropped for many years, was allowed to revert to its natural state when it attained the height of 58 feet.

The flowers are inconspicuous, and come out in Europe from March to May, according to elevation and latitude, the pale yellow anthers with their abundant pollen growing on one tree, the berry, acorn-like in form, growing separately on another. The fruit ripens from September to November of the year of flowering.

There are only four species, says Du Hamel du Monceau, one of which is common to Europe,

Asia, and North America (*T. canadensis*).[1] Parlatore[2] enumerates five species, two from Japan, three from North America, which Hooker regards as all forms of the same species. The other three are so similar in character that some botanists arrange them all under one species.[3] Asa Gray considers the Canadian form identical with that of Britain.

Several well-marked varieties exist, *e.g.* the 'Irish yew'—*Taxus baccata fastigiata*—first discovered about one hundred and twenty years ago on a mountain in the parish of Kellisher, near Florence Court, Co. Fermanagh, Ireland,[4] which, though so different in character, is only a variety of the common yew. Large specimens of the Florence Court yew exist in the gardens of Roebuck Castle, Dundrum—these are 20 feet high; two other fine ones grow at Grange-Con, Co. Wicklow, in the grounds of D. Mahoney, Esq. There is also a fine specimen at Ballynure, Clones, and an old place near this spot, called 'Gortgranard,' is famous for this form of yew. There are others of great size at Drumsillet House, Carrigallen. Mr. Veitch says,[5] 'the seeds always revert to the common type through being fertilised by the common yew.' Until lately no male plant of this variety had been met with,

---

[1] *Traité des Arbres*, 1768. [2] Brandis, *Forest Flora of India*.
[3] *Encyclopædia Britannica*. [4] *Gardener's Chronicle*, 1891.
[5] *Gardener's Chronicle*, 1873, and July 18, 1891.

but Mr. Tillett of Norwich[1] has produced one with male flowers. It is a well-known feature of the yew that it now and again becomes monœcious, *i.e.* having both male and female flowers on the same plant.

The upright form and the arrangement of leaves—peculiarities which characterise the *fastigiate* form—are really juvenile or seed-bed characters which have become persistent. Other varieties are *Taxus baccata procumbens* and the Neidpath yew, *T. baccata erecta*; *T. baccata fructu-luteo*, a variety with yellow fruit, first found in 1817 in an old orchard near Glasnevin, Dublin; *T. baccata aurea*, a beautiful golden-leaved plant, which is mentioned in Plot's *History of Staffordshire*, A.D. 1686, as a 'yellow-leav'd Yew Tree' occurring in that county; *T. baccata Dovastonii*, a pendulous form, which originated about a hundred years ago at Westfelton, near Shrewsbury; and *T. adpressa*, of which variety a tree, measuring 3 feet in girth, and having a diameter of shade of 30 feet, is found in the garden of the Earl of Annesley at Castlewellan, Co. Down.

Veitch gives a number of other varieties chiefly of horticultural interest.

The generic name *Taxus* is derived from the Greek τάξος, which, from τάσσω, 'to arrange,' has, very probably, reference to the two-rowed arrange-

[1] *Manual of Coniferæ.*

ment of the leaves; or it may refer to τόξον, a bow; or to *toxicum*, poison, the common yew being poisonous. It is more likely that τόξον, a bow, is derived from the name of the plant.

According to Dr. Johnson our word 'yew' is derived from the original Anglo-Saxon *Iþ*, or Welsh *yw*, but Dr. Price traces it to the Latin word *Iva*, which also includes the ivy. Mr. J. G. Cumming[1] gives the following meanings of the word yew:—' Yew is ancient British, and signifies *existent* and enduring, having the same root as Jehovah, and yew in Welsh means *it is*, being one of the forms of the third person present indicative of the auxiliary verb *bód*, to be.'

The various spellings show how much change the name has undergone:—

Eu (Chaucer, four times), *Ew* (thrice).
Eugh (Spenser), *Ewgh, Ugh,* and *U, Ewe* (Ascham), *Iuu,*[2] *Yugh, Yeugh, Yewe, Yowe* (Palsgrave), *You* (Brand, p. 71).

The synonyms are as follow:—

Greek, Μίλος.
Latin, *Taxus*, Virgil, Pliny, etc.
German, ⎱ *Eibe, Eibenbaum, Ibenbaum, Ifen-*
Swedish, ⎰ *baum.*

---

[1] *Notes and Queries,* 1st Ser. viii.

[2] Iuu is 'given as the spelling in the Epinal MS.' i. 44, and as this is the earliest MS. extant in English, and goes back to the seventh century, it may confidently be said to be the oldest spelling of the word extant in any Teutonic language.—*Notes and Queries,* 1887, vol. iv. p. 532.

YEW-TREE IN YEWDALE, CONISTON.
From a block kindly lent by the Editor of 'THE GARDEN.'

French, *If baccifère* (Du Hamel du Monceau), pl. 19, p. 61.
Italian, *Taxo*.
Spanish, *Texo, Iva*.
Portuguese, *Iva*.
Irish, *Whar*.[1]
Dutch, *Jeuen, Jeuenboom*.
Welsh, *Yweu, Yreu-yw*.
Gaelic, *An-t-iuchar*.

M. Lat., *Ivus, Iva* or *Ina*, 'a name which Dr. Price says was an abbreviation of *Ajuga*, a corruption of Abiga, a plant which Pliny considered to be the same as *chamæpitys* (χαμαιπίτυς), but which was also applied to several plants, and is of uncertain derivation.'

In *Notes and Queries*, 1887,[2] T. C. asks if *yews* were ever called *view* trees, and quotes several instances he has met with. Looking at the etymology of the term, it seems impossible that it can ever have been a customary spelling; it can only have resulted from *y* being mistaken for *v*, and from the odd changes in the value of *v* and *w*, such as may still be found in Norfolk, where it is not

---

[1] 'The name of the tree in Celtic is *jubar*, pronounced *yewar*, *i.e.* "the evergreen head." The town of Newry in Ireland took its name from two yew-trees which St. Patrick planted (!): *A-Niubaride*, pronounced *A-Newery*, *i.e.* the yew-trees which stood in Cromwell's time, when some soldiers ruthlessly cut them down.'—Fras. Crossley, *Notes and Queries*, 1st Ser. viii. 4481.

[2] 1887, vol. iv. p. 532.

uncommon to speak of the 'vine of the grape wine,' meaning the wine of the grape vine. An old quotation given in *Notes and Queries*,[1] attached to a commission, shows this spelling: 'I find the following, dated March 10, 1662 :—" Nottingham. An Inventory of the Goods and Chattells of Sr Jno Byron the elder, Knight, taken at Mansfyld.

'Item four Spanish viewe bowes wth a quiver and arrowes at . . . . . . xl^s" '

Another writer speaks of *vew* being common in the Craven district. This again is evidently dependent on *y* being mistaken for *v*.

An improvement suggests itself to some one. *Vew* is a prospect, which is not spelt without an *i*. Hence 'the yews' in Worsborough Dale become 'the views'! Halliwell in his Diet of archaic and proof words gives yet another form, *vewe*, which he says is a Cheshire word.[2]

Still another writer says there is a farm in South Shropshire named Yeo, which is always pronounced *View* by the people of the neighbourhood.

Epithets.—From the earliest times the epithets and adjectives used in connection with the yew nearly all link it with sorrow or death; and most of those of modern date are similar in character, or else mere translations. Thus we find such terms as these constantly employed :—*melancholy, funereal, mourner, black, dark, sable, stubborn, sullen, tough,*

---

[1] 1st Ser. vi. 10.   [2] *G. F. R. B.*, 1884, 6th Ser. vol. ix.

shooter, distinguished, pensive,[1] *mortifère, forceful* (Pope, *Iliad*), *ductile*. In Poole's *English Parnassus* we have the additional epithets: *warlike, dismal, fatal, mortal, venomous, unhappy, verdant, deadly, deathful.* Most of these are taken from old English poetry. Many are derived from the weapons the tree produces. Those of a funereal character are not so much due to the tree itself as to the purposes to which it has been applied, and the localities in which it is so often found. But, as Grindon justly points out,[2] it is man who has placed it in cemeteries and churchyards. Nature gives the yew a very different abiding-place, and perhaps after all it may prove to be a tree that should contribute ideas rather of hope than of mourning.

[1] 'The manly oak, the pensive yew.'—*Rokeby*, canto v. 13.
[2] *Trees of Old England.*

CHAPTER II

Geographical distribution—Indigenous—Geological remains—
Sparse distribution in England—Reasons for this.

THE yew has, according to Nyman,[1] a wide distribution throughout Europe, being found in Switzerland, Austria, Germany (Vosges, Jura, etc.), Holland, Norway, Sweden, Finland, Britain, France (Alps and Pyrenees), Spain (Pyrenees, Asturia, Grenada, Valencia), Portugal, Italy (Alps, Apennines), Sicily, Dalmatia, Croatia, Hungary, Transylvania, Caucasus, Greece, Russia. The tree is rare in Greece, though it is mentioned in the *Flora Græca*, on the authority of Mr. Hawkins, as being found on the rocks of Mount Cyllene in Laconia,[2] and by Theophrastus under the name Μίλος, as occurring in Macedonia. It must have been very plentiful at one time both in Germany and France, for Cæsar says: 'Magna in Galliâ, Germaniâque copia est;' but nowadays it is seldom seen in either country, except in the mountain districts. Mathieu[3] on this account was led to regard it as a species in its decadence, of which,

---

[1] *Sylloge Floræ Europeæ*, p. 348.   [2] Daubeny, p. 43.
[3] A. Mathieu, conservateur des Forêts, *Flore Forestière*, p. 444.

however, there is no evidence. Its disappearance from the intermediate districts is due to its destruction by man and not to natural dying out. 'Cette espèce,' he says, 'ne forme point en France de massifs forestiers ; ailleurs, elle n'en constate que très exceptionellement, toujours subordonnée et peu abondante, à stations très disjoints. Elle offre tous les caractères d'une espèce en décadence, qui, autrefois assez répandue, a une tendance manifeste à disparaître.'

It grows in the Western Himalaya beyond the Indus and on the Safed Koh at 5000 to 10,000 feet. Sir Joseph Hooker found it at Churra in the Khasia Mountains, and at Kala-panee at 5300 feet.[1] It does not, as a rule, grow higher than 40 or 50 feet, with 7 or 8 to 18 feet of girth. A few trees were observed at Kulu.[2]

Madden, however, records a tree at Gungutri 100 feet high and 15 feet in girth ; 5 to 6 feet is however the usual size in N.W. Himalaya.[3] Gamble measured two trees on Tonglo in Sikkim which gave :—

No. 1. Height, 30 feet ; to first branch, 10 feet ; girth, 20 feet.
No. 2.   „   70 „   „   30 „   „   16 „

It also grows in Japan and the Philippine Islands. Mr. W. Robinson informs me that he saw it

---

[1] *Himalayan Journals*, p. 268.
[2] E. Balfour, *Timber Trees, etc., of India*.
[3] *Manual of Indian Timbers*.

on Mount Babor in Kabylia in considerable quantity beneath the cedar forests at about 4000 feet. It is found in America at various elevations up to 4000 feet. In Great Britain its distribution, although fairly wide, is not so extensive as might have been expected. It was probably this fact, coupled with some ignorance of the amount of existing trees, which led the Hon. Daines Barrington to doubt whether the species is indigenous to Great Britain. He never saw the yew 'where it grew in great masses' or appeared to be sown by the hand of Nature, and he says that the most conspicuous groups are to be found on the Surrey Hills, but in scarcely any instance covering more than an acre, whereas at Cherkley Court, near Leatherhead, there are over ninety acres thus covered with fine old trees evidently sown naturally.

There are also large masses of yews in Kinglye Vale in Sussex; along the Wye at Tintern, and in Dovedale; on the rocks at Borrodale, and on Conzie Scar near Kendal, all which are truly natural stations. If a proof of its aboriginal character were needed, we have one in its having been found buried in peat-mosses of great age in Ireland,[1] and in those of Matterdale and Patterdale, where, accord-

---

[1] *Cybele Hibernica*, 1866. The yew is said to be found from south to north of Ireland, in upland woods and rocky places on mountains; rare in the wild state. Truly wild in the mountainous parts of the west and north.

YEW-TREE AT CHERKLEY COURT.
From a photograph sent by A. Dixon, Esq.

ing to Withering,[1] large pieces still retain their beautiful red colour. I have in my possession a spear-head made of this wood, which was dug from beneath the peat in the Fens of Cambridgeshire, and which may be fairly regarded as at least three or four thousand years old.

Professor Ramsay[2] shows that it is of far greater antiquity than this : 'In the forest bed which lies underneath the glacial deposits on the shore at Cromer, in Norfolk, *Taxus baccata* (yew), *Pinus sylvestris* (Scotch fir), and a number of other plants, are found associated with mammals, such as the elephant, rhinoceros, bears (four species),' etc. etc. 'This indicates a vast antiquity on the part of the yew, dating from pre-glacial times, when this country was united to the Continent, and a milder climate prevailed than at present.' He says it is also found in the Bristol Channel associated with the same kind of fossils.

Even this does not show its extremest age, since Professor Heer finds the yew-tree cones in the coal shale of Utznach and Dürnten, identical in form with those of the living plant, only somewhat smaller.

'Der Eibenbaum (*Taxus baccata*, L.).—Von diesem fand ich in Dürnten das Samennüsschen (Fig. 385), das in Form und Skulptur völlig mit dem lebenden Eibenbaume übereinkommt, nur ist

---

[1] *English Botany.*   [2] *Physical Geography of Great Britain.*

es etwas kleiner. Es hat einen rundlichen Nabel, eine ungemein feine runzlige Samenschale und vorn ein kleines, vorstehendes Spitzchen.'[1]

The age of the yew-wood found in the ruins of Nineveh is as nothing in comparison with this.

Although Barrington's doubt has no foundation in fact, it is somewhat singular that a tree which grows so readily in favourable situations should not be more widely spread and abundant in this country. The probable explanation of this is to be found, over and above the destruction of the trees for fuel, in the fact of its falling, during the time of snow, an easy prey to cattle, deer, hares, and rabbits, which eagerly feed on it when it is almost the only green food visible and has none of the holly's protective prickles. Under these conditions the only trees of this species which would have a chance of surviving would be those in enclosures or occupying inaccessible places among rocks.

Darwin[2] gives a very good instance of the manner in which trees are thus kept down by cattle :—

'At Moor Park I saw a rather pretty case of the effects of animals on vegetation; there are enormous commons with clumps of old Scotch firs on the hills, and about eight or ten years ago some

---

[1] *Die Urwelt der Schweitz.*
[2] *Life and Letters of Charles Darwin*, June 3rd, 1857, vol. ii. p. 100.

of these commons were enclosed, and all round the clumps nice young trees are springing up by the million, looking exactly as if planted, so many are of the same age. In another part of the common, not yet enclosed, I looked for miles, and not one young tree could be seen. I then went near (within a quarter of a mile of the clumps) and looked closely in the heather, and there I found tens of thousands of young Scotch firs (thirty in one square yard) with their tops nibbled off by the few cattle which occasionally roam over these wretched heaths.'

A similar state of things is found on the island of Inch Lonaig, where there is an extensive natural forest of yew. No young trees have sprung up for ages, as their growth is prevented by a herd of deer which has been introduced there.

Yew-trees are found in larger quantity on the rugged scars and clefts on the sides of hills than on low ground. How far this is due to peculiarities of soil, or drainage, or to the degree of protection they find there from the ravages of animals, through their more inaccessible position, it is not easy to say. Thus, on the Kent and Surrey downs, where they occur in lines or in large masses, the former may be the explanation, while in some of the Welsh valleys, in the valley of the Wye, at Tintern and in Dovedale, where the trees grow in profusion amongst the rocks, the latter reason may have more weight.

Then there is, perhaps, another reason to be found in the number of birds—blackbirds and thrushes—which come to feed on the berries, and after feeding fly to the rocks or hill-sides as resting-places. Thus, I noticed at Tintern that such resting-spots were covered with large quantities of the seeds; and as these places were always on a higher point than the tree on which the berries grew, it seems not unreasonable to suppose that the lines of yew-trees on the Kent Hills may have arisen through this habit.

The Pilgrim's Way from Winchester to Canterbury, graphically described by 'Julia Cartwright' (Mrs. Ady), points to a very general distribution of the yew over an extended area.

'Once more upon the hills,' she says, 'we can follow the line of yews which are seen at intervals along the ridge from Saint Martha's Chapel, by Weston Wood and the back of Albury Park—turning a few steps out of our path to visit Newland's Corner, one of the most beautiful spots in the whole of Surrey.

'Some of the oldest and finest yew-trees in Surrey are close to Newland's Corner. The ancient yew grove there is mentioned in Domesday, and their dark foliage offers a fine contrast to the bright tints of the neighbouring woods, and to the snowy masses of blossom which in early summer clothes the boughs of the gnarled old hawthorn-trees that are studded over the hill-side.

YEW-TREE AT ALBURY PARK, SURREY.

'So striking is this feature, and so fixed is the idea that some connection exists between these yew-trees and the Pilgrim's Way, that they are often said to have been planted with the express object of guiding travellers along the road to Canterbury. This, however, we need hardly say, is a fallacy. Yews are by no ways peculiar to the Pilgrim's Way, but are to be found along every road in chalk districts' (p. 6).

It is not improbable that these parts of the country were at one time covered with yew-trees, and that those along the 'Pilgrim's Way' have escaped destruction, and been left as guides.

'It has been suggested, by Capt. E. R. James, that the Pilgrim's Way first gave Bunyan his idea of the *Pilgrim's Progress*' (*ib.*).

The remarkable paucity of very large trees in Ireland, where the yew abounds and grows with great luxuriance, may be due to two causes, viz., 1st, the very humid climate, causing rapid decay, and, 2nd, the destruction of the woods for smelting and other purposes. Thus: 'In ancient times,' says Boate,[1] 'and as long as the land was in full possession of the Irish themselves, all Ireland was full of woods on every side, as evidently appeareth by the writings of Giraldus Cambrensis, who came into Ireland upon the first conquest in the company of Henry the Second, King of England, in the year

[1] Dr. George Boate, *Ireland's Natural History*, 1758.

of our Saviour eleven hundred and seventy-one.' And he goes on to explain how the English diminished the woods, 'partly to deprive the Theeves and Rogues of their refuge and starting-holes,' and partly for turning the ground into good pasture land. In later times they were destroyed, partly for being made merchandise of in the form of pipe-staves, and for making charcoal for ironworks. And Hayes observes:[1] 'The year 1692 introduced into *Shillela* that bane of all our timber, iron forges and furnaces, and as the parties were allowed to fell for themselves several thousand cords of wood yearly, and were only confined to a particular district, they cut whatsoever was most convenient for the purpose.'

In a similar manner, Ralph Thoresby, writing in 1703, accounts for the disappearance of the woods in the Forest of Knaresborough. This, he says, 'did abound with *minera ferri*. It was once so woody, that I have heard of an old writing, said to be preserved in the parish chest of Knaresborough, which obliged them to cut down so many yearly as to make a convenient passage for the wool-carriers from Newcastle to Leeds. Now it is so naked that there is not so much left for a waymark.' And in his Diary (A.D. 1694) he says that iron ore was taken from Cumberland to Ireland to be smelted.

[1] *Treatise on Planting.*

CHAPTER III

Age of yew-trees—Considered slow-growing—Mode of estimating age—Traditional accounts—Age of contiguous buildings—De Candolle's method of calculating age—Rings of growth—In young trees, correct—In old, erroneous—Rejuvenescence—Increase by welding of young shoots—Variable growth.

WE owe to De Candolle, the great Swiss botanist, some of the erroneous views which are prevalent as to the extreme age which this tree is supposed to attain.

He held that there are no set limits for the duration of the life of trees, and he arrived at the conclusion that, were it not for the results of accidents or disease, there is no natural cause by which a period is put to their existence. But the same might be said of some animals under similar conditions, and indeed there is a very close analogy between the growth of a yew-tree and that of a coral.

In his mode of estimating age, however, he assumed that the tree's growth took place by a regular deposition of concentric layers, which, except in the case of young yews, is very wide of the truth, and hence calculations founded on this assumption are found to be very fallacious.

'It is not, as commonly stated, Malpighi, but the

ingenious Michel Montaigne, who has the merit of having been the first, in 1581, in his *Voyage en Italie*, to notice the relation of the annual rings to the age of the tree. (Adrien de Jussieu, *Cours élémentaire de Botanique*, 1840, p. 61.)

'A skilful artist, engaged in the preparation of astronomical instruments, had called the attention of Montaigne to the rings, and he also maintained that the rings were narrower on the north side of the tree.'[1]

The yew-tree has hitherto been regarded as the most slowly-growing, as it is undoubtedly the most durable, of all trees. It 'appears to me,' says De Candolle, 'of all European trees, to be that which attains the greatest age.' But while it is true that they have reached an age of centuries, the dates assigned to them are, in many instances, absolutely fabulous.

Traditional accounts are untrustworthy, and of historical records there is scarcely a reliable one to be found which exceeds two hundred years. Records of this kind, 'when reliable,' may, as De Candolle suggests, 'throw light on the history of ancient buildings, as these may in turn throw light on the age of the trees.' The latter suggestion has been largely acted on in this country, with results which are often most unsatisfactory, and sometimes even absurd, as will be shown later.

[1] Humboldt, *Aspects of Nature*, vol. ii. p. 94.

De Candolle says that we may consider a tree from two points of view; either as an aggregate of individuals or as a single being :—

'On peut considérer un arbre sous deux points de vue; ou bien on peut dire qu'un arbre est un agrégat d'autant d'individus soudés ensemble, qu'il est développé de bourgeons à sa surface; ou bien on peut le considérer comme un être unique. Dans la première manière de s'exprimer, qui est probablement la plus rationelle, on ne peut pas s'étonner si de nouveaux bourgeons s'ajoutant sans cesse aux anciens, l'agrégat qui en résulte n'a point de terme nécessaire à son existence.'[1]

And he goes on to say, justly enough :—

'On conçoit sans peine qu'il peut se glisser des erreurs dans les calculs de ce genre . . . la vie de l'homme est bien courte pour de pareilles recherches' (p. 4).

He then proceeds to calculate the age of yew-trees, which, during the greater part of their life, certainly after 150 to 200 years, are 'aggregates of individuals' as single trees.

He found from the measurement of two trees of the known age of 71 and 150 years, that the rate of growth was one inch of radius in $25\frac{1}{2}$ years, and on this basis he calculated that the Fortingall tree in Perthshire had attained the age of 2500 to 2700 years in 1770, about the date at which it was visited

[1] *Notice sur la Longévité des Arbres*, 1831, p. 6.

by Pennant,[1] who speaks of the 'remains of a prodigious tree 56½ feet in circumference.' The Hon. Daines Barrington,[2] who also paid a visit to it, says, in a paper read at the Royal Society: 'I measured this yew twice, and therefore cannot be mistaken when I inform you that it amounted to 52 feet. Nothing now remains but the outward bark, which hath been separated by the centre of the tree's decaying within these twenty years. What still appears, however, is 54 feet in circumference.'

De Candolle[3] also makes mention of the Brabourne tree as of almost equal age, and remarks: 'I venture to indicate these trees to botanists and foresters, that they may authenticate them, and establish, if possible, their law of increment; for it is probable that they are the veterans of European vegetation.'

'Ceux de l'ancienne abbaye de Fontaines près Ripon . . . avaient en 1770, d'après Pennant, jusqu'à 1216 lignes de diamètre, ou plus de douze siècles.

'Ceux du cimetière de Crow-hurst, . . . 1283 lignes ou . . . quatorze siècles et demi.

'Celui de Fotheringall[4] en Ecosse, avait en 1770 un diamètre de 2588 lignes et par conséquent vingt-cinq à vingt-six siècles.

---

[1] *Tours in Scotland*, 1771.   [2] *Phil. Trans.* 1769.   [3] *Bibl. Univ.* ii. 66.
[4] See *Fortingal* for an amusing error due to this mis-spelling.

YEW-TREE AT CROWHURST, SUSSEX.

'Celui du cimetière de Brabourne, comté de Kent, avait en 1600 . . . 2880 lignes, et s'il existe encore il attendrait 3000 ans.'

YEW AT FOUNTAIN'S ABBEY.
After STRUTT.

Two trees, or a single tree, as some think, in Kyre Park, Worcestershire (*q.v.*), well illustrate the way in which an erroneous impression of extreme age may arise. Two immense trunks are growing close together, the one being 30 feet in girth at the ground-level and the other 36 feet at the same point. It is probable that these have either originally formed one trunk and have split asunder, or they have been two trees growing closely together. Had their tops been broken and young shoots started from the base, the trees would have been considered as one, beyond a doubt, and the girth would have far exceeded that of the Fortingal tree.

De Candolle's method of estimating the age by the number of annual rings, gives, in young trees with undecayed centres, fairly accurate results, except in those instances where there is more than one centre, but it can of course be applied only in the case of trees which have been cut down. The age of certain trees calculated in this manner proves them to have passed many centuries. Various species of conifers have thus been shown to have as many as 300 to 1000 annual rings. *Sequoia gigantea* is said to have reached 1500 to 2000 years, and *Sequoia sempervirens* 1300 to 1750 years. The latter, however, resembles the yew-tree in some particulars, and notably in putting out shoots from the base when the central trunk is destroyed. These soon grow into large trees, and even coalesce, so that in time there will seem to have existed a tree of extraordinary girth. I have seen instances in California where large trees, cut down as recently as 1848 or 1849, are now surrounded by a circle of trees 50 to 60 feet in height, inside which the assemblies of the infant colony were held.

It has been questioned whether some of these trees may not produce more than one ring in a year. In this country it is certain that only one annual ring can be produced in young trees, but then it seldom happens that a yew exceeds two hundred years without having the main stem injured by storms or disease, and it is impossible beyond this period to depend upon the number of rings as a test of age.

In young trees which have not been injured, and in which the trunk remains sound, the number of annual rings represents their age. This is true of those which under the same conditions have reached the age of two hundred years, and even somewhat beyond this period.

Thus, in a tree of the known age of two hundred and forty years, which was cut down on Inch Lonaig, Loch Lomond, Sir Robert Christison and Mr. Gordon counted 237 rings in the longer, and 227 in the shorter diameter. In another tree 227 rings were counted, but in this instance there were three separate centres, a fact of great importance, indicating that three separate branches or trunks had become welded together. Beyond the age of 200 to 250 years this method is no longer reliable, for at this period the tree has attained its full growth as a single trunk, and in the majority of instances decay or fracture has taken place, and coincidently with either of them a series of remarkable changes in rejuvenescence.

Whenever the leading shoot or main stems of a yew are broken, all the wood of that portion of the trunk with which they are connected dies. The bark coverings of the tree do not die, but at once put forth a vast number of young shoots. If these are deprived of light and air by overshadowing branches, they die back and a fresh crop ensues. This also happens if the shoots are eaten by cattle. The swollen bases of these young shoots are covered by the spread of the bark, giving rise to bosses or a thickening which may extend in part or wholly round the trunk. If the top of the tree is completely destroyed, the young spray grows thickly all round the remaining portion of the trunk. The shoots attain a considerable growth, and become welded together, and in this way there arises a rapid increase in the tree's girth. The smaller shoots thus enveloped by the spread of the bark produce a vast number of rings, which are eventually concentric, and in a measure resemble annual rings, which they are not, as several or even many of them may be produced in a single year. This explains how in 'a yew that was dug up in a bog in Queen's County, and which was proved (?) to have been 545 years of age, it had grown so slowly during the last three hundred years of its life that *near the circumference* 100 rings were traceable within one inch.' Yew-trees are apt to become more or less unequal on opposite sides, owing to a variety of causes, such as greater exposure on one side to frost or cold, winds or snowstorms, causing fracture, or difference of soil. In this way many trees not only show an eccentric arrangement of their annual rings,[1] and a difference between the two sides, but they may also differ on the same horizontal level on the same side. Bowman's observations on the Darley Dale Yew show a variation of thirty-three to sixty-six rings in an inch of radius. A tree may have died on one side, or may have ceased growing, while the other side is growing vigorously. There may be a period during which the tree grows scarcely at all, but after the top is broken, rejuvenescence takes place, and rapid growth ensues.

It is not only the young shoots that are welded by the spread of the bark. The wounds left by large branches having been cut off or broken, and even exposed surfaces of dead wood which has lost its bark, may become sealed over by a polyp-like growth, and further decay prevented by their becoming hermetically closed. The old tree at Crowhurst, Surrey, shows very strikingly how this kind of action has conduced to its preservation.

---

[1] One mentioned by Sir R. Christison had its centre twice as distant from one side as from the other. This tree was only 24 inches in girth.

Very large branches cut off after being broken by a storm more than forty years ago have now their cut surface almost perfectly cicatrised.

In Ireland the lopping off great boughs seems, contrary to what is found in England, to cause general decay of the tree, as is seen in the case of the Great Yew of Glendalough, or Seven Churches, County Wicklow.

Writing in 1794, S. Hayes, of Avondale, says:—

'There was within these fifty years a single yew-tree, adjoining one of the Seven Churches in Glendalough, from whose lofty trunk, about 16 feet round, extended on every side a mass of close branches, which shaded from the sun, and sheltered from every inclemency of weather the picturesque ruin it adorned, and all the churchyard. This I have had from the indubitable authority of several who still remember it. When in its full beauty on a hot summer's day, at a time that numbers were regaling themselves under its shade, a gentleman of the party, who pleaded the authority of an agent to the See (but whose employer, I am persuaded, could not have ever viewed the scene), had all its principal limbs and branches sawed off close to the trunk, *for the value of the timber.* From that time to the present, which may be about forty years, the poor remains have been in a constant state of decay; it has scarcely put out a branch, the bark has fallen off, and a large holly is growing up through the fissures of the stem; so that I consider it too far gone to enumerate it amongst the large trees still standing in the county of Wicklow.'

This shows the effect of a moist climate, and in a measure helps to explain the disappearance of old trees in Ireland—rapid decay following on the mutilation, which in England would have produced a crop of young shoots from the trunk and a rejuvenescence of the tree.

The rate of growth in trees of several kinds varies at different times, and it is found that the number of annual rings represents a widely divergent degree of growth. Thus De Candolle himself counted the rings in several oaks, and found that one which had attained the age of two hundred years had only the same circumference as another that had reached fifty. It is well known also that the rate of growth is not uniformly diminished, for he found one oak of 333 years which had increased as much between 320 and 330 as it had between 90 and 100. These observations on the oak apply with equal force to the yew. It is not uncommon in the latter to find the tree developing more on one side than on the other, as is shown in a specimen in the Kew Museum, where 250 rings are found on one side and 50 on the other.

Comparing the number of annual rings with the number of lines of radius, De Candolle considered that for trees of 150 years the annual growth somewhat exceeded a line of diameter, and in those of 150 to 250 years that it was less than this.

'Si pour les ifs très âgés on admet la moyenne d'une ligne par an, il est probable qu'on est au-dessus de la vérité, et qu'en estimant le nombre de leurs années, égal au nombre de lignes de leur diamètre, on les fait plus jeunes qu'ils ne sont.'

It should be borne in mind that a line of diameter means only half a line for the thickness of each annual ring which represents the amount of radius, or half the diameter. The trees on which De Candolle's estimate was founded were evidently stunted and ill-grown, making the rate of growth much too low, as has been shown by the evidence of well-formed trees. The calculation of the age of old trees, such as those of Fortingal and Brabourne, on this basis, is entirely fallacious.

CHAPTER IV

Rate of growth—Point of measurement—Sir R. Christison's view—Objections—Instances—Measurements of trees of known age—Increase at fixed points and at stated periods—Examples—Dr. Christison's and Dr. Beddoe's measurements—Mr. Bowman's method—Trephine—Objections—Traditional accounts—Fallacies—Rate of growth in old trees—Periods of rest and growth.

BEFORE considering the rate of growth, it is necessary to fix on the point of measurement. Christison[1] thought that the lowest level is the only suitable spot for comparative measurement, 'because the annual growth of the rings of wood increase in width in a progressive ratio upwards, owing to the gradual increase of the swelling under the division of the trunk into its lowest limbs.' This is in part, but not altogether true. The swelling is due mainly to the welding of the lower shoots together, and not to the division of the trunk, which is quite another thing. He says, further, that the ground-line is fortunately the right place, 'for most aged yews' have their trunks so

[1] *Trans. Bot. Soc. Edin.*, 1879.

deformed by knobs and excrescences that they cannot allow of a comparison anywhere else, and that the stem is so covered with young spray that it is difficult to pass a measuring-tape round it, except at the ground. To this it may properly be objected that in trees such as those at Dryburgh, Roseneath, Yattenden, Sanderstead, and many similar ones elsewhere, the swell of the roots is so great that measurement at the ground-line would make the age appear to be greater than it really is—in some instances as much as one-third; whereas in other cases, as that of Darley Dale, the increase at the ground-line in sixty years is *nil*, while the trunk has grown beyond the rate of young trees. There is in trees grown in churchyards another objection to this point, viz., that the ground-level is continually rising. On the other hand, trees growing in exposed situations often have the soil scraped away by animals and the roots exposed. For these reasons the ground-line is very unreliable. The best point of comparison is at 3 feet from the ground; but in practice it is as well to take the ground-line in addition.

The following Table gives a number of examples of the ground-line yielding a larger girth than the higher level, and proves that this is not the best point for measurement :—

SUNSHINE AND SHADE, YEW TERRACE, CASTLE WARD, DOWNPATRICK.

From a photograph sent by LADY BANGOR.

Table of Girth Measurements at level of the ground and at 3 feet.

Puckington	Ground 13·0 feet,	at 3 feet	11·0
Yattenden	,,	11·0	,, ,,	9·6
Trentham	,,	33·6	,, ,,	17·6
Stoke Gabriel	,,	15·0	,, ,,	5·0
Tisbury	,,	31·0	,, ,,	30·6
Brockenhurst	,,	21·0	,, ,,	18·0
Stowting	,,	22·6	,, ,,	20·8
,,	,,	19·6	,, ,,	17·5
Northiam	,,	19·0	,, ,,	18·6
Mamhilad	,,	30·9	,, ,,	29·10
Goytre	,,	32·4	,, ,,	22·0
Iffley	,,	25·0	,, ,,	22·0
Church Preen	,,	40·5	,, ,,	21·9
Stoke Courcy	,,	15·0	,, ,,	10·6
Portbury	,,	17·3	,, ,,	15·10
Hambledon	,,	39·0	,, ,,	14·0
Icklesham	,,	19·0	,, ,,	15·6
Kyre Park	,,	30·0	,, ,,	24·0
,,	,,	36·0	,, ,,	32·0
,,	,,	30·0	,, ,,	26·0
Roseneath	,,	15·0	,, ,,	11·2

It is preferable, as a rule, to take measurements at both these points.

Passing on to the question of rate of growth in yew-trees, we have two methods by which this can be arrived at :—

1. By the measurement of trees of known age ; and
2. By the measurement of increased girth at a fixed point and at stated periods.

In trees of known age the rate of increase varies considerably according to locality, climate, and soil. In some cases a foot of diameter is produced in sixty years, or even in a shorter period, in others in seventy-two to eighty. The late Sir R. Christison thought that a foot in seventy-five years was about the average rate of growth, but many English trees far exceed this. Unless we are to believe that these grow more rapidly than Scottish trees, his estimate would appear to be too low. Good examples of the relation of known age to girth are to be found in an avenue of yew-trees at Tytherly (in Queenswood), Wilts, consisting of 120 trees, averaging about 24 feet high, with trunks nearly 2 feet in diameter.[1] These were planted 120 years ago, so that they represent a growth of nearly 1 foot of diameter in sixty years. The eighteen young trees in Gresford Churchyard, near Wrexham, measured by Mr. Bowman, and of which the age was known, from the parish records, to be 120 years, had attained a diameter of 21 inches, or 1 foot of diameter in nearly $68\frac{1}{2}$ years. But by far the most remarkable data which have hitherto been recorded are those mentioned in the *Times* by Mr. Walter Money, and repeated by Professor Henslow in *Nature*, October 24, 1889, with accurate measurements. From this account it appears that the parish register records the

---

[1] Loudon, *op. cit.*

Instances of rapid Growth

planting of a yew-tree in Basildon Churchyard by Charles, Lord Fane, in 1726. In 1780, fifty-four years afterwards, this tree measured 6 feet 3 inches near the ground, which is an extraordinary rate of growth, supposing the top to have been unbroken. Allowing four years as the age of the tree when planted, the rate of growth in this instance equals 1 foot of diameter in twenty-four years.

Two remarkable instances of rapid growth are to be seen in the Churchyard of Boughton-under-Blean, near Faversham. These trees are stated in the parish register to have been planted, the one in 1695, the other in 1840. The former measures 9 feet 9 inches in girth at 3 feet from the ground, being at the rate of a foot of growth in 61·5 years; the latter having increased to very nearly the same amount in 54·1 years.

The trees at Winterbourne, of the known age of 172 years, have a diameter of 3 feet and 2 feet respectively, giving a rate of growth 1 foot in 57·3 and 86 years.

At Old Meldrum Manse, Aberdeenshire,[1] two trees, believed to have been moved to their present site in 1680, now measure 10 feet and 10 feet 2 inches respectively.

At Camperdown, Forfarshire, a tree planted in 1816, which has grown very vigorously, is now 3 feet 10 inches in girth at 3 feet from the ground,

[1] *Trans. Roy. Arboricult. Soc.*, vol. xii. part 3.

a rate of increase which gives 1 foot of diameter in a little over fifty-two years.

At Parkhill, near Blairgowrie, is an old yew-tree with a girth of 15 feet at 5 feet from the ground.[1] It measures at the ground 14 feet 5 inches, and was 'probably planted in 1610.' This would make it 280 years old, yielding 1 foot of diameter in fifty-six years. By Sir R. Christison's calculation of 1 foot in seventy-five years the age would appear as 375. One at Pitmedden,[2] in the same county, which was planted in 1675 by Sir A. Seton, is now 10 feet 8 inches at 3 feet from the ground. The rate of increase in this case is very nearly 1 foot of diameter in sixty-one years.

At Hurstbourne Tarrant, near Andover, there are two yew-trees in the churchyard, one being 8 feet 4 inches, the other 7 feet 3 inches, in circumference. The Parish Register thus records their planting. Of the former it says :—

'The ewtree near to the vicar's garden planted by Sam: Hoskins (vicar) in ye year 1693.'

It is thus a little over two hundred years old.

The latter is 155 years old, as appears from the Register :—

'Memorandum : Oct. 10, 1741. There was an yew-tree planted in the churchyard pretty near the outward rails. By the order and at the

---

[1] *Trans. Roy. Arboricult. Soc.*, vol. xii. part 3.
[2] Hutchison, *op. cit.*, 1890.

expense of James Wilkins, M.A., Vicar of this parish.'[1]

The second kind of measurement was inaugurated by the late Sir Robert Christison,[2] and has been continued by his son, Dr. Christison.[3] The results are of great interest and value in determining the rate of growth in young trees. Thus 'No. 47' was noted in 1878 'as having a smooth trunk of about 5 feet, unpruned, but overshadowed by other trees on one side. The annual average growth in the last nine years was only 0·09, its rate for the previous sixty-four years of its life having been 0·53. No. 48 showed that its annual increase for sixty-four years down to 1878 was 0·59, and since then has been 0·48.' No. 49 'stands clear upon grass.' 'Its annual increase for sixty-four years was only 0·37, but in the last nine years it has averaged 0·45. The average annual girth-increase of six is 0·38. Removing two whose girth-increase has received a prolonged, though, judging from their healthy appearance, not probably a permanent, depression from the severe frosts of 1879, 1880, and 1881, the average of the remaining four rises to 0·44. These four trees are known to be seventy-two years old, and they yield an average girth of 36 inches and a diameter of 12·3, which is beyond the usual rate of growth (?),

[1] W. P. W. Phillimore, *Notes and Queries*, Ser. 8, vol. x.
[2] *Trans. Bot. Soc. Edin.*, 1879.   [3] *Ibid.* vol. xix.

and is no doubt due to favourable conditions of soil,' etc. 'No. 41, a beautiful spreading yew, by far the largest in the garden, is *traditionally* believed to have been transplanted in 1767 from the old Physic Garden to the Botanic Gardens in Leith Walk, and is known to have been transplanted thence in 1821-22.' 'By traditional history it must be 190, and may be 240.' 'This yields an annual rate of 0·35 in the first case and 0·28 in the second.' 'Even the highest seems low for a tree of such a healthy vigorous look as this, and it is probable that the traditional history is at fault.' 'If the growth of the last ten years be taken as an index, the age would be about 180; but Dr. Christison's measurements of the four trees, Nos. 47, 48, 49, and 50, prove that the growth of the last nine years, which, as above mentioned, gives ·44 girth-increase per annum, or (at the rate of) 11·73 of diameter in eighty years, is below the actual increase, which amounts in the known period of seventy-two years to 12·3 inches, whereas on the above rate of ·44 it would have been only 10·28 in that time. So that there is reason to believe that the rate of No. 41 is also below the average in the last nine years.'

I am indebted to my friend Dr. Beddoe, F.R.S., for some measurements of three trees growing in his grounds at 'The Chantrey,' Bradford-on-Avon :—

Rate of Growth

	1892.		1893.		1894.		1895.		1896.		
	Apr. 1.	Nov.	Mar.	Nov.1.	Mar.	Nov.1.	Apr. 1.	Nov.1.	Apr. 1.	Nov.1.	
My Yew-trees.	33·3	33·6	33·55	33·7	33·8	33·8	33·8	33·9	34·	34·3	1 in. in five yrs.
	40·	40·7	40·7	...	41·5	42·	42·1	43·1	43·1	44·	4 ,,
	17·8	18·6	18·6	19·1	19·1	19·8	19·8	20·6	20·6	21·2	3·4 ,,

Of these trees, the first is completely overshadowed by a large beech-tree, and is on a dry rocky site. They all show a very slow rate of increase.

The Table shows an almost complete cessation of growth from November to March.

A yew-tree at Wellow, East Somerset, was planted in 1834 and was then 'the size of a finger.' It measured in 1882, 38·5 inches; in 1896, 43·7 inches (I. B.).

The growth of this yew has been about 42 inches of circumference in sixty-two years, and 5·2 inches in the last fourteen. 'It does not look a very thrifty tree.'

The increase is at the rate of 14 inches of diameter in sixty-two years.

In the following Table examples are given of the best instances of known age in England:—

Rate of Growth in Young Trees.

	Planted.	Diameter.
Tytherly . . .	120 years	2·0 feet
Basildon . . .	163 ,,	2·1 ,,
Gresford . . .	120 ,,	1·8 ,,

	Planted.	Diameter.
Boughton	200 years	3·3 feet
,,	45 ,,	1·3 ,,
Winterbourne (A)	172 ,,	3·0 ,,
,, (B)	172 ,,	2·1 ,,

In Loudon's *Arboretum* we have the following:—

	Planted.	Diameter.
Gosford House, Haddington	35 years	1·3 feet
Minto	140 ,,	2·0 ,,
Coul, Cromarty	200 ,,	2·6 ,,
Monboddo	100 ,,	2·0 ,,
Kinnaird Castle	35 ,,	1·8 ,,
Taymouth	100 ,,	2·0 ,,
Charleville Forest	45 ,,	2·0 ,,
Down, at Castle Wood (King's Co.)	134 ,,	2·8 ,,
Florence Court	89 ,,	3·0 ,,
Jardin des Plantes, Paris	120 ,,	1·8 ,,
Avranches, Botanic Garden	40 ,,	1·0 ,,
Willemshoe, Cassel	30 ,,	1·0 ,,
Vienna, Univ. Bot. Garden	30 ,,	9 ,,
Berlin, Sans Souci	45 ,,	11 ,,
Tabley Hall, Cheshire	70 ,,	1·0 ,,
Southend, Durham	28 ,,	1·0 ,,
Donnington Park	35 ,,	10 inches
Melbury Park, Dorset	200 ,,	3·0 feet

In Scotland (Hutchison):—

Pitmedden, Aberdeenshire	220 years	3·1 feet
Parkhill, Blairgowrie	280 ,,	4·9 ,,
Old Meldrum Manse	215 ,,	3·4 ,,
Camperdown, Forfar	79 ,,	1·3 ,,
Ochtertyre, Perth	90 ,,	1·8 ,,
Rosslyn	195 ,,	2·11 ,,

Calculating Age by the Trephine 57

Excluding those figures which are doubtful or obviously incorrect, and assuming the remainder to be accurate, they give a ratio of growth of 1 foot of diameter in about fifty-six years,—a much higher rate of growth than that arrived at by Sir Robert Christison.

A third mode of computing the age of yews, by means of the trephine, which Mr. Bowman used, in old trees is, I believe, of no utility whatever, owing to the fact that the external rings are not regularly concentric and formed in the ordinary manner of young trees, but are due, as I have shown, to the aggregation of many young shoots, thus giving rise to a far greater number of rings than would result from annual growth alone. In the Darley tree, for instance, Mr. Bowman found by this method that the increase amounted to 1 inch of radius in forty-six years, whereas the actual increase of girth in the last fifty-two years, at 2 feet from the ground, amounts to no less than 3 feet 2 inches or 1 foot 8 lines of diameter in the same period, which is a very rapid growth. Mr. Bowman was himself evidently not quite satisfied with his observations. They led him to think that 1 line a year is too little to allow, and that De Candolle's average 'makes old trees too young and young trees too old.' For the latter he would allow 2, and in the case of trees growing in rich soil 3, lines a year till they had attained 2 feet in diameter, when, with De Candolle, he would allow 1 line.

Age deduced from tradition and proximity of ancient buildings.—It is never safe to trust to computations from traditional accounts. There is always an unconscious tendency to exaggerate the age of certain objects, which through their great antiquity become, as the narrator supposes, more wonderful or more venerable the older they are made to appear. Abundant evidences of this tendency are to be found, not only amongst classical writers, but amongst those of more recent times.

The doubtful character of traditional accounts cannot be more strikingly shown than in the case of the Abercairney tree in Perthshire, which is said to have at one time sheltered the Marquis of Montrose. The tree is 10 feet 7 inches in girth at 5 feet from the ground, a point when it divides, and is therefore probably not much over two hundred years old. Between 1640 and 1890 two hundred and fifty years have elapsed. The tree, if it existed, must have been very small at the former date, and could scarcely have afforded much shelter.[1]

The practice of ascribing to a tree the age of an adjacent building, so common in the present day,

---

[1] 'Old and Remarkable Yew-trees in Scotland,' *Trans. Royal Scot. Arb. Soc.*, 1893.

is due to a suggestion of De Candolle. It would be hardly worth while to notice this method were it not so frequently practised by men of intelligence. To show the absurd deductions to which it may lead, there are in Kent two contiguous parishes, the churchyards of which have each a large yew, the one 16 feet and the other 17 feet in girth. The churches are eleventh and fourteenth century, so that there would in this way be three centuries of difference.

A similar fallacy is evident in the case of Arbuthnot,[1] where a tree in the manse garden, with a girth of 8 feet 11 inches, is thought by Mr. Hutchison to date from 1242, in which year the Church of St. Ternan, near which it stands, was consecrated by Bishop de Bernham. Thus we should have an increase of diameter of only 35 inches in 648 years, or very nearly 1 foot in 216 years, a rate of growth opposed to all proved data. The Boughton tree attained a greater size than this in two hundred years. We should not forget to note that nearly all estimates of age ignore the relative sizes of the trees, so that we find two trees of the same dimensions may differ five or six hundred years in estimated age, which is a palpable absurdity.

At Arngomery, Stirlingshire,[2] there is a tree

---

[1] *Trans. Royal Arb. Soc.*, 1890.
[2] 'Old and Remarkable Yew-trees in Scotland,' *Trans. Royal Scot. Arb. Soc.*, 1893.

measuring 10 feet 4 inches at 3 feet from the ground. A note says: 'Old buildings taken down lately near the site of trees were of eleventh century.' This tree is less in girth than that at Pitmedden, known to be planted in 1675. The age of the buildings, therefore, is no guide to that of the tree.

'Tradition,' says Mr. Farrer,[1] 'would seem to contain nothing incredible when it asserts that the yews on Kinglye Bottom, near Chichester, were on their present site when the sea-kings from the North landed on the coast of Sussex.' Had he said that 'yews were there' the statement would have been accurate, but that 'the yews,' meaning those still existing, were then in being, is too large a demand on our credulity, as there is no tree at that place which exceeds 15·4 in girth, or possibly about five hundred years in age.

Tradition is again at fault in the case of a tree at Yew Park, Clontarf, Co. Dublin, where there is a fine specimen, 12 feet in girth, of which the owner, H. Brougham Leech, Esq., LL.D., writes: 'It is not surrounded by young shoots; it presents the appearance of a tree in the midst of a small plantation.' (The dense shade thus produced sufficiently explains the absence of shoots on the trunk.) 'The branches project horizontally, and touch the ground, and then, without taking root, strike upwards again.

[1] *Longman's Magazine*, 1883.

The circumference of the shade is 76 yards. . . . About forty or fifty years ago a portion, including part of the trunk, fell out owing to the weight of snow after a snowstorm.' 'Tradition would make it nearly 900 hundred years old, and says that Brian Boru, king of Ireland, died under it at the battle of Clontarf, in which he defeated the Danes on Good Friday, A.D. 1014.' This would make it 983 years old, while the girth is only 12 feet.

Rate of Growth in Old Trees.—De Candolle assumed that after a certain period the rate of growth diminishes, and he accounts for this by the greater distance of the roots from the air, by their coming into contact with the roots of other trees, or with a rocky or unsuitable soil, or by the diminished elasticity of the bark.

The trees on which his observations were founded were evidently of unhealthy and stunted growth, arising probably from defects of soil or climate. His ideas, however, on the rate of growth have been adopted by most subsequent writers and taken *au pied de la lettre*. But more extended observation and certain measurements of recent times lead to the belief that these ideas and the inference deduced from them are erroneous. It will be shown presently that, as regards the yew especially, there is ground for the assertion that not only does its growth not diminish with age, but that on the contrary it increases, on the whole, with a rapidity as great as, and in many instances much greater than, that of young trees.

Sir R. Christison held with De Candolle that there was diminution of growth in old trees, but then he took as the proper point of measurement the ground-line, which, as I have shown, leads to considerable confusion. Thus, at this point, the Darley Dale tree had made no growth whatever during fifty-two years, while at a higher spot the increase much exceeded that of young trees. There is, however, in many old trees an occasional arrest of growth which may last over a long period. The Ankerwyke tree, near Staines, for instance, which in 1882 measured 27 feet 8 inches, in 1877 had reached a girth of 30 feet 5 inches; 2 feet 9 inches in fifty-five years, or 11 inches of diameter, which exceeds the average growth of young trees. Since then there has been an arrest of growth, as the increase in 1894 was only 4 inches, or 16 lines, of diameter in seventeen years. This is explained by the greater part of the nourishment going to the internal trunk.

Mr. R. Hutchison[1] mentions a tree (one of fifteen) at Ellon Castle, Aberdeenshire, which has increased in the last thirty-six years 5 feet 6 inches in girth at 1 foot from the ground. This gives 22 inches of diameter in that period, or 1 foot in 19·8 years, an amount of increase far exceeding any recorded measurements.

[1] *Trans. Royal Arb. Soc.*, 1890.

Rate of Growth in Old Trees

The Ormiston yew is another instance of growth in mature age as great as that of young trees. Mr. Hutchison considers this tree second only to the Fortingal yew in point of age, size, and historical interest. Of this last I would say nothing. Historical interest has found such a wide field of conjecture in old trees that one can only admire the fertility of speculation with which they have been invested. Norbury Park and Cherkley Court, however, can show many trees of greater age and size. The Ormiston tree measured, in 1834, 12 feet 9 inches at the ground, and 17 feet 8 inches at 5 feet. In the forty-five subsequent years it had gained at the rate of 1 inch radius in twenty-two years at the ground, and 1 inch in twelve years at 3 feet, and 1 inch in eleven years at 5 feet, the two latter measurements giving a rate of increase very nearly 1 foot of diameter in seventy-two and sixty-six years respectively.

A tree at Ferniehurst Castle, Roxburghshire,[1] which measures 10 feet 7 inches at 2 feet from the ground, 'is supposed to be five hundred years old.' It is difficult to understand the reasons for assigning such an age as this, which seems to be mere guess-work, seeing that the same writer mentions those of Old Meldrum and Pitmedden as having nearly the same diameter, though they are known not to be much more than two hundred years old.

[1] Hutchison, *op. cit.*

In the same manner the tree at Blairgowrie, having a girth of 14 feet 5 inches, is mentioned as 'probably planted in 1610.'

Although there is abundant evidence to show that old trees grow at intervals much more rapidly than young ones, they do not, as I have said, grow uniformly, but have periods of comparative arrest of growth. This occurs in trees which have formed a good overshadowing head, beneath which the young shoots cannot grow on the trunk. . As soon as any part of this head is broken, which it probably is every half-century or so, rapid growth of the trunk sets in. Most trees of good age afford evidence of this kind—having all the branches of a much slighter age than would be indicated by the trunk. If then the two periods of growth and arrest be taken together, we may fairly assume that the average rate of growth of old trees at least equals, and generally exceeds, that of young ones. Without some rule, warranted by actual observation, we are apt to form very erroneous ideas of the age of these trees. From the data already obtained it would appear that the average rate of increase is from 1 foot of diameter in from sixty to seventy years—both in young and old trees. It may be even more rapid than this, but I think it better to take the lowest estimate, and for this reason prefer to adopt Sir R. Christison's estimate, for purposes of calculation, of 1 foot in seventy-five years, though there is every reason to believe that this is considerably below the average rate of growth.

It is worthy of note that the cypress planted at Chartreux by Michel Angelo was 13 feet in girth in 1817, giving an average rate of girth-increase of over 4 feet in the first three centuries. The rate of increase in diameter for the whole period is 1 foot in 69·7 years, a growth nearly as rapid as that of the yew.

CHAPTER V

Causes of variation in growth—Retardation and acceleration—Pollarding—its meaning—Frequency—Causes—Results—Rings of wood—Hollow trunks becoming solid.

THE rate of growth in yew-trees is very variable,—at one time becoming so slow as to seem, to the ordinary observer, altogether arrested; at another period growing with a rapidity far beyond that of the usual rate of increase.

All the conditions which conduce to variation require somewhat minute consideration before we can arrive at an approximate idea—and all estimates of this kind can only be approximate—of the age of any of these trees.

First, then, of

Pollards.—The conditions on which pollarding depend are of several kinds, but a word or two is necessary as to the meaning of the term 'pollard,' which, in the case of the yew-tree, must be taken to mean the breakage, or cutting, or even the bending, of the leading shoot. Bacon says: 'Nothing procureth the lasting of trees so much as often cutting; and we see all overgrown trees are pollards or dottards, and not trees at their full height.' If an ordinary tree lose its leading shoot, it is generally reproduced quickly, and frequent cutting is thus necessary to form a pollard, but it is not so with the yew. If the leading shoot be injured, it is seldom that a secondary lead is formed, but rather a head of branches of equal size. This is due to the immense number of leaf-buds which exist on every shoot. As many as sixteen to twenty of these may be counted in the length of an inch. It will appear presently what an influence this fact has on the growth of the trunk.

It is remarkable that we scarcely ever see a yew-tree of good size growing with a single lead. I only know of two or three which have this character, one at Dunkeld, another at Rokeby, and a third in the churchyard at Portbury, near Bristol. In most other instances it would seem to have been destroyed or injured, and if the trees are carefully examined the remains of the original trunk will be readily discerned. The condition resulting from this kind of injury is practically the same as that from pollarding. That is to say, there ensues a distinct swelling of the trunk, along which new shoots are thrown out in large quantity, just as occurs in trees which are really pollarded, and if the tree is growing in the open, and has branches down the trunk, these enlarge at the expense of the top, and thus produce an unequal thickening of the stem.[1] The causes which produce injury of the lead or main stem differ in kind and degree according to the age of the tree. Thus in the young state it may have been eaten off by animals; at a later period it may have been cut by man for the manufacture of bows, as Keats makes Endymion say—

> 'I'll poll
> The fair-grown yew-tree, for a chosen bow.'

At a still later period it may have been riven by lightning or broken by a wind-storm such as that which did so much damage to the famous Borrodale yews in December 1883.[2] More destructive still are heavy falls of snow, which not only split off large boughs, but in some instances demolish an entire group of trees. In the winter of 1886 more than seven magnificent trees were thus destroyed in

---

[1] Mr. Fernow gives the following description, which may serve as a type of what occurs in a conifer after fracture: 'Let a tree grow up under favourable conditions for a hundred years, as the Douglas spruce in question seems to have done, when its ring-growth will be wide, its crown reaching above its neighbours. A hurricane breaks off a large part of its crown, when necessarily and suddenly, at least within a year, the rings become narrow in proportion. Within the next thirty years the crown recuperates, which, in a resinous conifer like the Douglas spruce, is possible without fear of fungus attacks and decay; but the food-material descending from the foliage will for a long time be only sufficient, on the particular section in question at the base of the tree, to make a narrow annual ring, even after the crown is fully recuperated. Were a section cut higher up in the tree, it would be found that the rings there have begun to widen sooner than at the lower section. Finally, and rather suddenly for any given section, the supply has become normal, and especially if an exceedingly favourable season occurs at the same time the rings show again normal width.'—B. E. Fernow, *Nature*, May 28, 1896.

[2] Described by the Rev. H. Drummond Rawnsley in the Wordsworth Society's *Transactions*.

YEW-TREES IN BORRODALE.

the grounds of Mr. A. Dixon at Cherkley Court in the middle of the unrivalled grove of yew-trees which flourishes there. In the same snowstorm some fine trees in the Druids' Grove at Norbury were much injured. In one instance all the upper boughs of a large tree were broken off, while the lower ones were all bent down to the ground, and remained permanently in that position. The trunks of these trees are now densely covered with young spray..

Overcrowding, as a reason for diminished rate of growth, appears in the investigations of Professors Hartig and Weber.[1] 'In those trees which, owing to close crowding in the forest, have only developed feeble crowns, the annual increment is greatest just beneath the crown, and diminishes regularly downwards; and in very closely-crowded trees . . . the ordinary mode of ascertaining the age of the tree would yield false results, for the number of annual rings at 3 or 4 feet high is less than the number of the tree's life. The physiological meaning of the above is, that the small leaf-area does not supply sufficient food-material to provide for the needs of the whole sheet of cambium, and the upper parts take all that is sent down, leaving none for those below.' In those which have well-developed crowns the rule is exactly converse. 'If such trees as the above are suddenly exposed to full light and air by cutting

[1] 'Das Holz der Rothbucke,' *Nature*, March 28, 1889.

down the neighbouring trees, the annual rings on the lower parts of the stems suddenly become much broader; no such stipulation of the increment occurs in the upper part.'

Frosts are sometimes very injurious. Du Hamel du Monceau[1] says that yews suffered in France much damage from the frosts of 1709, and Malesherbes found several killed by the severe frost of 1789.

Galls affecting the growth of Yews.—Selby states that yews are remarkably free from the attacks of insects;[2] but next to wind and snow one of the most injurious agents in certain localities is a species of gall (*Cecidomya taxi*).

Loudon says:[3] 'Both the wood and leaves being poisonous, neither are attacked by insects, or, if they are, it is in a very slight degree. The points of the shoots, in some situations and seasons, produce little tufts of leaves, which may be considered as abortive shoots.'

These abortive shoots are due to the insertion of the eggs of a gall-fly (*Cecidomya taxi*, Inchbald) at the extreme tip of the young shoot, causing an arrest in the growth of the shoot, the leaves being developed in the form of a cone. In this cone the number of leaves amounts from fifty to seventy, or exactly what would have been produced had the

---

[1] Pp. 26, 302.   [2] *British Forest Trees*, p. 384.
[3] *Arb. and Frut. Brit.*, vol. iv. p. 2091.

year's shoot grown to its full length of two or three inches. This gall insect was first described by Mr. Inchbald in 1861. The pupa stage is reached in April or May. In June the orange-coloured fly

YEW AFFECTED BY GALLS.

appears. The length of its body is five millimetres in length, and the expanse of its wings nine millimetres.[1] It was formerly supposed that the pro-

[1] *Entom. Weekly Intelligencer*, 1861, vol. v. pp. 76, 77.

duction of galls was due to a minute quantity of poison introduced by the gall insect, but this view is no longer tenable. Dr. Adler[1] has shown conclusively that there is no foundation whatever for this supposition, and Beyerinck has proved that the fluid ejected by the gall-fly is without taste or smell, and absolutely unirritating if injected under the skin. It is probably nothing more than 'a very mild antiseptic' dressing applied to the wound made in the plant. Both these authors show that it is not in the gall-mother but in the larva that we must seek for the cause of gall-growth. These galls are, in some districts, exceedingly abundant; notably in Gloucestershire and Somersetshire, in Kent and in Windsor Park. Farther north they are much less frequent; while in Scotland they are unknown.[2] Not only is the opinion held by Loudon and Selby, that the yew is seldom attacked by insects, untrue, but there are instances which show that no tree suffers so disastrously from their attack. At Tintern, on the Wyndcliffe, in May 1889, I found most of the trees largely affected by galls. In some instances every twig had its terminal rosette, and it was apparent that this invariably led to the death of the shoot, as the tree was covered with the dead twigs of several years and was almost destitute of foliage;

---

[1] *Alternating Generations: A Study of Galls*, etc. Translated by C. R. Straton, F.R.C.S.
[2] *Auct.* Prof. Trail.

the only healthy shoots remaining being formed as a dense spray on the upper surface of the main branches. The ground under the tree was here and there covered with the little rosettes or cones which had been bitten off by birds (probably titmice), in every instance the larva having been extracted.

At Dinder, near Wells, I saw, some years ago, a number of trees about 15 feet high and 3 feet in girth at the base, planted about sixty years ago, all much infested by *Cecidomya* on their upper branches, which were stunted and unhealthy-looking, while the lower branches, which were almost free from galls, were well-grown and vigorous. The whole tree showed one of the marked effects of pollarding, viz., rapid growth of the lower trunk and branches.

If we examine into the results following injuries of the main stem, or more important branches, produced by the causes above mentioned, we find that all the remaining part of the trunk or branch below the site of injury generally dies at once, with exception of its coverings, the bark and its underlying liber and cambium layers. These latter begin to form a new ring of wood enclosing the old dead trunk, creeping over and covering up cut or broken surfaces. This process has been likened, with a good deal of force, to the necrosion of a shaft of a bone, and its inclusion in a new bony case produced by the periosteum. The simile is in many respects a striking one. The bark, which contains the germs of buds or its substitute, immediately begins to put forth a profusion of young branches over its whole surface parenchyma. Between these there ensues a struggle for existence; a few acquire superiority in growth, and the rest die for want of air and light. In the meantime the swelling of the bases of the young shoots has caused them to become welded together, and thus the trunk becomes largely thickened. The branches, which have acquired the pre-eminence, generally to the number of three or four, begin to form a new head, and occasionally are found uniting to form a new trunk. But the head may be again destroyed and the new trunk killed, and both may be again reproduced as at first. In this way, three or even four, concentric rings may arise, the inner ones being dead and the outer ones living. A striking illustration of the result of injury to the primary trunk is to be seen at Court Lodge, near Shorne, in the grounds of Mr. Isaac Winch. The central trunk, which is a foot in diameter, was broken off, probably by the fall of another tree, at 7 feet from the ground, being at this time (1889) about seventy years old. At 4 feet from the ground it is surrounded by a vigorous growth of boughs, some of which measure 8 inches in diameter. The circumference of the new trunk at this point is 9 feet. If we take this girth as repre-

Effects of Fracture of Trunk 75

senting the age of the tree, it would appear to be 225 years old. But as the central foot of diameter was produced in about seventy years, and the two outer feet must have grown in the same space of time, we have 140 years as the real age. In all probability, nay, almost certainly, it was much less than this, for the oldest branch only measured 8 inches in diameter, and therefore could only have reached fifty years of age, giving for the total age 125 years, or 100 years less than would be found by ordinary reckoning. Another tree near the same locality has been broken off about 2 feet above the ground; a series of large branches springing from the base surrounds the trunk. When these have grown another fifty years, they will probably show a girth of 12 feet, giving an apparent age of 300 years instead of 125, which would then be the real age. The amalgamation or welding together of so many young shoots around the broken trunk leads to a very rapid increase in girth. It is obvious that the growth of new stems on opposite sides of the trunk, whether consisting of single trunks or a number amalgamated together, must grow at least at the same rate as an independent trunk, and therefore the two sides of the tree will together produce a given thickness in half the time which a single trunk would demand.

To illustrate this, we may imagine a trunk to

have attained the age of seventy-five years, and therefore a diameter of 12 inches. The trunk becomes fractured, and then produces a ring of young shoots. After each of these has grown for a further period of seventy-five years it will also have attained a diameter of 12 inches. We have thus a total diameter of 36 inches, or one-third more than would be produced at the ordinary rate of increase, and representing therefore an apparent age of 225 years instead of 150 years, the actual age.

Three yew-trees in Llanbedrog Churchyard, near Pwllheli, well illustrate the effect of early destruction of the stem, and serve to show how such trees as that at Fortingal may have arisen. No. 1 is 21 feet high, and out of its stem, which is nearly on a level with the ground, eight trees grow and make one bush. No. 2 has twelve trees growing in a similar manner, and No. 3 has five.

The Rectory tree at Maynooth, having no stem, but a fine head 26 feet high, and spreading 55 feet in diameter, and the Pant Chudw tree in Wales, which has a girth at the ground of 30 feet, and spreads 84 feet, are also good illustrations of compound growth. Another example is to be seen at Llanvihangel-Generglen, Cardiganshire, where twelve boles spring together from the ground.[1]

The Irish yew affords a good illustration of the effects of quasi-pollarding. Some of the oldest

[1] *Gardener's Chronicle*, 1880.

trees of this interesting variety are, according to Loudon, at Comber in the County Down. They are supposed to have been planted before 1780. In 1838 one of these had attained the height of 21 feet. The circumference of the trunk at 1 foot from the ground was 4 feet 5 inches. This gives an increase of 14·1 inches in fifty-eight years, which is largely in excess of that of the common form, and is evidently due to the peculiar form of arrested growth by which the full expansion of the tree is curtailed and the trunk thickened as in a pollarded tree.

A still more striking instance of the influence which arrested upward growth has in causing thickening of the trunk is to be seen in the case of two trees of this variety mentioned by Loudon as existing at Nether Place, Ayrshire. These must have been about the same age as the preceding, *i.e.* planted about 1780. They both had their tops cut away, and as a result had put out fifty-six and sixty-six branches respectively, having a circumference varying from 6 inches to 2 feet. The trunks girthed 9 feet and 8 feet, or nearly three times the average rate of increase of well-grown common yews. The age of these by De Candolle's reckoning would appear as 432 and 384, instead of 110 years.

Rings of Wood.—It is not uncommon to find a dead central trunk enclosed in old yews. Round this there may be two or three concentric rings of wood. The inner one or two may also be dead. Thus, the Darley Dale tree displays three inner rings of dead wood, as does the Bredhurst tree, and that at Dinder.

An imaginary section of the Bredhurst yew shows the formation of four distinct rings of growth. Some trees in Norbury Park, a section

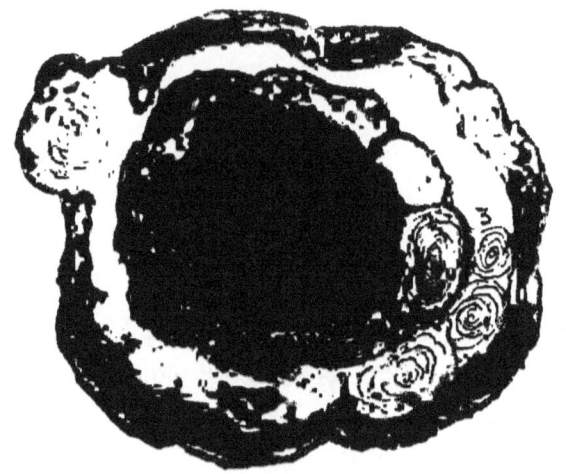

SECTIONAL VIEW OF YEW-TREE IN BREDHURST CHURCHYARD, KENT.

of one of which is given, show how these rings may have been formed by the coalescence of the young stems produced around and after the death of the main stem. One of the secondary stems has also died; and, after its disappearance by decay, and after the union of the remaining stems,

Rings of Wood

there would result an opening to the central stem, such as we often find in old trees. Near Tintern

SECTIONAL VIEW OF YEW-TREE IN NORBURY PARK.

there are several trees showing this peculiarity in growth. One of these is especially noteworthy as exhibiting what I have never before seen — the simultaneous growth of two rings after the death of the main stem, which has a diameter of 1 foot. The circumference of the outer circle is 15 feet, and in sixty or seventy years the individual

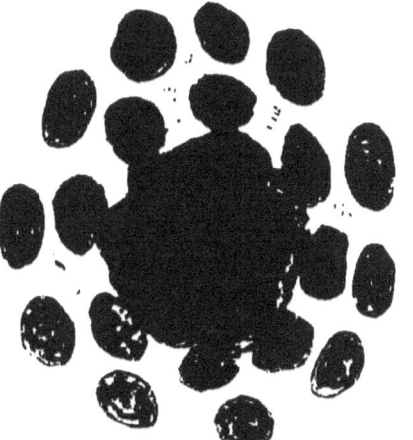

SECTIONAL VIEW OF YEW-TREES AT TINTERN.

trees of each circle may all coalesce. We should then have an apparent age of 450 years, for, by that time, the girth would have increased to 18 feet. Mr. Hutchison (*op. cit.*) mentions a similar fact as occurring on Inch Lonaig, Loch Lomond. 'Many of these yews,' he says, 'when they have begun to decay, have sent up shoots close to the old trunk. A number of these coalesce and form at last a complete new trunk, inside of which the old one continues to decay.'

Trees becoming solid through the formation of roots in the centre—Dinder, Mamhilad, Portbury, Ankerwyke, Kyre, Llanthewy-Bach, Stanstead, Bettwys-Newydd, Breamore, etc.—are apt to show a diminished rate of increase, or even complete arrest of growth, owing to the fact that the major part of the nutriment is carried by them to the tree, and thus the increase takes place within, and the external growth is correspondingly decreased. In some instances a large cavity has become solid through this kind of growth. In the case of the Mamhilad tree, a distinct central trunk has formed, attached to the outer part by two or three narrow connections.

CHAPTER VI

Notable trees and their measurements—in England and Wales—in Scotland and in Ireland—All trees of 10 feet in girth and upwards—Trees of 30 feet in girth and upwards in England and Wales.

THE following list includes all trees having a girth of 10 feet and upwards :—

Place.	County.	Girth at ground level.	Girth at 3 feet.	Length of Bole.	Height.	Diameter of umbrage.	Remarks.
		Feet.	Feet.	Feet.	Feet.	Feet.	
Aldworth	Berkshire	19	27 27·3	10 (Loudon)	...	24	This tree, in the churchyard, has not grown since 1760. 'Now a ruin' (Rev. W. L. Newham).
Clieveden	,,	16	18	7	...	...	1896.
Hampstead Marshall	,,	47	...	...	...	...	37 ft. girth in 1836 (Loudon).
Bucklebury	,,	...	27	...	...	...	In 1806 (Lysons).
*Watcombe	,, (A)	...	20				
	,, (B)	...	10				
Vattenden	,,	11	9·6	...	30	...	In churchyard 1889 (J. L.).
Newbury Hedsor	Bucks	...	27·0	...	...	...	This tree is mentioned in 1805 by Lysons, but had ceased to exist in 1836.
Medmenham	,,	10·7	11·8	2·10	49	38	'Not hollow; no spray' (Rev. W. Hill).
Llangeitho Churchyard	Cardigan (1)	...	14	9	50	49	'No shoots. Hollow, holding ton of coal for church purposes.'
	,, (2)	...	16	7	58	43	Hollow.
	,, (3)	...	14	8	56	40	Do.
	,, (4)	...	16	10	55	38	'Not hollow; but shoots from ground.'
Pantllydw	Carnarvon	30	18	Nil.	52·6	84	'A good many young shoots, where branches have been broken off' (Col. Ruch).
Bettws-Newydd	,,	30·6	...	...	...	...	Internal root of large size (Gard. Chron., Feb. 17 1877).

* Those marked thus * are referred to in chap. xii.

F

Place.	County.	Girth at ground level.	Girth at 3 feet.	Length of Bole.	Height.	Diameter of umbrage.	Remarks.
		Feet.	Feet.	Feet.	Feet.	Feet.	
Llandegai	Carnarvon	11·1	8·11	11·9	50	48	'Not hollow; no young shoots' (Rev. D. Jones).
Penrhyn Park	,,	17·6	14·2	3·0	57	59	Some hollows, and decayed wood where branches were broken in the storm of 1887 (W. Lester Smith).
Gyffin	,, (A)	14	12	7	31	44	1896 (Rev. T. R. Ellis).
	,, (B)	13	12	4	32	36	Do. do.
Caerhun	,, (A)	22	19	4·6	50	65	Not hollow; partly surrounded by young shoots.
	,, (B)	14	17	5	38	51	Do. do.
	,, (C)	19	19	1·6	36	60	Do. do.
							1896 (Rev. J. W. Roberts).
Haworth Castle	Cumberland	...	at 4 ft. 15·11	11	55	...	Trunk decayed.
Lanercost Churchyard	,, (1)	...	14	12	...	...	Hollow, broken at 15 feet, forming a new head.
,,	,, (2)	...	at 4 ft. 11	...	38	...	Trunk a shell.
*Gresford	Denbigh	at 2 ft. 23	at 4 ft. 27·6 at 5 ft. 29·0	...	52	...	In 1878. Male.
Chirk	,, A)	11·0	10	4	26	40	Hollow, much young spray.
	,, (B)	13·6	10	10	30	34	Not hollow, do.
	,, (C)	15	15	6·6	22	30	Hollow, do. Five others—girth from 7·6 to 9·9 (Rev. E. J. Evans).
*Darley Dale	Derby	at 27	2 ft. 4 27·7	...	...	...	Measured by Mr. Bowman, 1836.
		27	30·9	...	...	...	Mr. Paget Bowman, 1888.
Allestree	,,	17·6	17·8	7·6	33·6	53	Hollow, surrounded by young shoots (Rev. A. West, 1896).
Manaton	Devon	...	13	...	40	70	1892 (J. L.).
Stoke Gabriel	,,	15	5	6·10	40	83	1836 (Loudon). 1895. 'Not hollow, no spray' (Rev. F. H. N. Neville).
'St. John in the Wilderness,' Withycombe	,,	...	30	...	...	...	A compound tree (Gard. Chron., Jan. 1878).
Abbott's Leigh,	Dorset	22	24	...	...	...	1889, in churchyard (I. L.).
Shortgrove	Essex	15·9	...	...	...	...	Loudon, 1836.

THE PATTERDALE YEW.

From a photograph by A. PETTIT, *Keswick.*

Place.	County.	Girth at ground level.	Girth at 3 feet.	Length of Bole.	Height.	Diameter of umbrage.	Remarks.
		Feet.	Feet.	Feet.	Feet.	Feet.	
Overton	Flint	17.3	16.1	5.2	35	36	'Hollow' (Rev. J. W. Unwin, 1897).
*Westbury-on-Trim	Gloucester	12	15	...	...	...	1892 (J. L.).
Schowle, Forest of Dean	,,	30	...	...	...	...	*Gard. Chron.*, May 30, 1870.
*Henbury	,,	12.6	...	...	...	...	1892 (I. L.).
Hambledon	Hants	17	18	8	...	35	The late Rev. T. White.
Corhampton, Bishop's Waltham	,,	22	25	6	42	57	Female (Rev. H. R. Fleming).
*Brockenburst	,,	21	18	...	36	70	Girth 15 ft. in 1793; height 60 ft. (Loudon). Height 45 ft. in 1895. This is Sir T. D. Lauder's 'Lymington' tree.
Breamore	,,	...	30	...	...	...	Has 8 or 10 young trunks—a foot or more in diameter—growing within the old trunk (Shore, *Notes and Queries*, 1888).
Northington	,,	...	13.6	...	...	...	In churchyard. Original central stem 3 ft. in diameter in 1890.
*Dibdin	,,	...	30	...	...	...	'Above roots' (Sir T. D. Lauder). Disappeared before 1866 (Miss Carlyon).
Long Sutton	,, (A) (B)	26.7 15.5	...	...	...	...	In churchyard, 1895 (Rev. W. Standen).
Warblington	,,	26	30 at 5 ft. 33	8	60	60	Rev. W. B. Norris. Fem. 26 ft. at 3 ft. in 1836.
Candover	,, (A) (B)	...	10 16	...	...	...	In an avenue ½ mile long, varying from 8 to 16 ft. in girth, 1890 (I. L.).
Hardham	,,	21 in 1835	...	...	...	...	Horsfield; destroyed by storm, 1840 (Rev. J. W. Sandham).
Selborne	,,	23.2	25.3	7.3	55	83	Gilbert White says: 'In 1789 was apparently of great age. The body was short, squat, and thick, and girthed 23 ft., supporting a large head. It was a male' (Loudon). 'Solid up to 5 ft., no young shoots' (Rev. Arthur Kaye).

Place.	County.	Girth at ground level.	Girth at 3 feet.	Length of Bole.	Height.	Diameter of umbrage.	Remarks.
		Feet.	Feet.	Feet.	Feet.	Feet.	
South Hayling	Hants	35	32.4 Dec. 1896	...	...	63	Diameter of dead centre, 8 to 10 ft. Tree hollow and covered with young shoots from the ground; trunk split at about 4 ft. Three years ago the girth was 31 at 4 ft.; difference caused by the split, 1896 (Mr. H. F. Trigg).
Bedhampton	,, (1) E. end of church	...	20.4	...	50	51	Hollow.
	,, (2) S. of church	...	20	...	50	54	Central dead trunk.
Steep	,, (1)	...	at 4 ft. 19.8	6.6	...	...	Hollow, bulging trunk.
	,, (2)	...	12.2	8	...	...	Clear, straight stem (J. James, Esq., 1895).
*Broxbourne	Herts	...	19.3	...	...	...	1896 (J. L.).
Peterchurch	Hereford	28	...	...	...	...	Woolhope Trans.
*Boughton-under-Blean	Kent	...	9.9 at 4 ft.	...	...	44	Planted in 1695.
			11	...	...	60	Rev. J. A. Boodle.
*Speldhurst	,,	...	18.6	...	25	...	Top broken; galls numerous, 1893 (J. L.).
Detling	,,	...	16	...	...	...	,, ,,
Kidbroke	,,	...	10.6	...	...	40.54	1838 (Loudon).
Petham, near Canterbury	,,	22.6	23.1	11.6	51.6	...	Sound; has young shoots surrounding it, 1896 (Rev. G. Stokes).
*Ulcombe	,, (A)	...	35.2	17	17	...	Girth at 17 ft. from ground 10.3 (Rev. J. Lampline, 1889).
	,, (B)	...	26.3 at 4 ft.	6	...	...	East end of church.
	,, (C)	...	20.5	...	...	...	
	,, (D)	...	12	...	...	...	
Capel	,,	...	27	6	...	...	Rev. F. Frost.
*Stanstead	,,	23.7	25.7	...	26	57	1892 (I. L.).
Thurnham	,,	17.2	23.8	8	...	28	Ch. circ. 1480 (J. L., 1889).
Detling	,,	...	17.6 at 4 ft. 18.4	10	...	54	Centre dead, 1889 (J. L.).
*Bredhurst	,,	...	21.6	...	...	...	1886 (J. L.)
Tudesley	,,	20.4	19.2	3.9	35	46	'Hollow: many young shoots' (Rev. G. L. Lachlan, Feb. 1897).

In England and Wales

Place.	County.	Girth at ground level.	Girth at 3 feet.	Length of Bole.	Height.	Diameter of umbrage.	Remarks.
		Feet.	Feet.	Feet.	Feet.	Feet.	
Harrietsham	Kent	...	30	...	...	...	Rev. J. Durst, 1889.
Charing	,,	...	12·6	...	...	...	,,
*Leeds	,,	28	32·6	...	...	...	A mere shell, 1892 (J. L.).
*Buckland	,,	24	...	...	...	25·30	In 1822 (Strutt).
Stowting	,, (A)	22·6	20·8	14	44·7	56	Female, opposite church porch.
	,, (B)	19·6	17·5	6·9	47.2	58·6	Female, opposite chancel, 1895 (Rev. A. Upton).
*Northiam	,,	19	18·6	7	...	25	'Perfectly hollow, and split in several places. It appears that a fresh trunk has grown from the ground' (Mr. Seeley, 1895).
Cudham	,, (A)	...	28				
	,, (B)	...	28·4	...	...	...	Rev. Nigel Freer.
*Braburne	,,	...	...	...	...	...	This grand tree, though long extinct, is inserted here to record its vast dimensions. It measured 58 ft. 6 in. in girth at the time of Evelyn.
Lamberhurst	,,	25	24	5	47	50-54	'Not hollow' (Rev. J. Langhorne).
Bidborough	,,	...	13·6	8·0			
*Shorne	,, (A)	at 2 ft.	12				
	,, (B)	...	17				
*Ankerwyke	Middlesex	25	30·9 at 7 ft. 35	14	...	74	May 24, 1894 (J. L.).
*Harlington	,,	17·1	19·6	8	80	65	In churchyard (Rev. E. J. Haddon, 1895).
Llanlellyd	Merioneth	18	...	...	...	...	In churchyard, 1891. Two trees about same size; the tops have been broken, and they are evidently compound trees.
Bala	,, (A)	18	18·6	6·6	40	51	'Hollow. Stem clear' (Rev. Th. Lloyd).
	,, (B)	about	same	size	...	...	
*Tintern	Monmouth A)	17·9	...	...	...	...	In the churchyard. Wyndcliffe.
	,, (B)	15·6	...	...	...	...	
Raglan	,,	12·8	...	...	30	...	In churchyard, 1894 (I. L.)
*Llanthewy Bach	,,	31	32·5	5	...	...	Trunk covered with spray, 1895 (Rev. W. A. W. Evans).
			30·4	...	...	...	Strutt, Sylv. Br., 1822.
*Mamhilad	,,	30·9 15 to 20 ft.	29·10 ...	7·6 ...	40 ...	65 ...	Rev. Ch. Cook, 1895. 'There are five others from 15 to 20 ft. in girth.'

Place.	County.	Girth at ground level.	Girth at 3 feet.	Length of Bole.	Height.	Diameter of umbrage.	Remarks.
		Feet.	Feet.	Feet.	Feet.	Feet.	
Goytre	Monmouth (A)	32·4	22	6·8	...	59	'Trunk not hollow, a little growth of young spray on one side' (Rev. D. T. Davies).
	,, (B)	30·4 at 4 ft.	...	...	...	53·7	
Llanfoist	,,	32	...	...	...	...	*Gard. Chron.*, 1874.
Hartburn	Northumberland	...	16·6	...	38	30	1836 (Loudon). 'Was destroyed 50 years ago by another tree falling on it. The remains of the trunk show that it must have been about the size given' (Rev. J. A. Kershaw, 1895).
Watcombe	Oxford (A)	...	10	...	...	...	1895. Letter in *Times*.
	,, (B)	...	20				
*Iffley,	,,	25	22 at 2 ft. 20 ft. in 1836	7	25	28	1895, Rev. H. Walmisley. 'Supposed to be coeval with church, prior to Norman Conquest'! (Loudon).
Maeslaugh Castle	Radnor	...	11·3	...	26	66	Loudon, 1836.
Kinlet	Shropshire	...	15	...	40	17	Loudon. The Rev. H. Case writes, 1895: 'There is no tree at Kinlet.'
*Church Preen	,,	40·5 at 1 ft. 30·10	21·9 at 4 ft.	...	50	61·6	'Hollow, interior measures 3 ft. 6 in. across' (Arthur Sparrow, Esq., 1895).
*Dinder	Somerset	...	31				
*Puckington	,,	13	11	7	50	63	'Trunk solid—planted in 1724, as shown in parish records' (Rev. W. H. Box).
*Broomfield	,,	24·4	16	4	...	39	'Hollow, surrounded by young growth' (Rev. P. G. Bulstrode, Jan. 1895).
*Ashill	,, (A)	14·7	15	6·7	...	...	Rev. Charles Houghton, 1895. 'One 15 ft. circ.' 1791 (Collinson's *History*).
	,, (B)	17·9	20	5·0	43	37	
Buckland St. Mary	,,	12	15·6	6	...	45	A.D. 1791. '12 ft. at 4 feet from ground' (*ibid.*). 'Not hollow, spray on one side' (Rev. W. Lance, 1895).
Stoke Courcy	,,	15	10·6	...	...	...	Collinson says it was a large tree in 1791. 'A dead shell only remains' (Rev. F. Meade King, 1895).

In England and Wales

Place.	County.		Girth at ground level.	Girth at 3 feet.	Length of Bole.	Height.	Diameter of umbrage.	Remarks.
			Feet.	Feet.	Feet.	Feet.	Feet.	
Allerton	Somerset		...	16	...	...	...	'Trunk filled in with brickwork; tree still vigorous and beautiful' (Rev. J. Gilbert, 1894).
Creech St. Michael	,,	(A)	18·3	18·10				
	,,	(B)	11·11	17	...	...	...	Rev. J. Bownes.
*Portbury	,,	(A)	...	16·7	...	...	...	Near gate of churchyard, 1889, hollow, central roots.
	,,	(B)	17·3	15·10	...	...	...	A fine undivided trunk of about 20 feet.
Leigh Court	,,		11	...	...	45	48 ⎫	
Brockley Hall	,,	(A)	18	...	...	...	... ⎬	Loudon, 1838.
,,	,,	(B)	17	...	...	...	... ⎭	
*Trentham	Stafford	(A)	16·3	13·6	...	...	... ⎫	Hollow.
	,,	(B)	12·9	12·3	...	...	... ⎬	Rev. E. Pigott.
	,,	(C)	33·4	17·6	.		... ⎭	
Himley Hall	,,		...	...	...	...	...	'Several immense trees' (Loudon).
Tettenhall, Wolverhampton	,,		24	...	...	...	...	Gard. Chron., May 30, 1874.
Aldbury	Surrey		...	22	...	...	...	1890 (J. L.).
Wotton	,,		...	18	...	...	...	,, ,,
			...	22	...	...	81	,, ,,
Windlesham	,,		...	12	...	...	...	Hone's *Every-day Book.* Blown down Dec. 1894. Had been many years dead (Mrs. Freshfield).
*Sanderstead	,,	(A)	11·6	12	...	...	61	Hollow (Rev. H. L. Maud, 1895).
				12·8				
,,	,,	(B)	15	14	10	65	78	,, ,,
*Hambledon	,,	(A)	36·1	39	14	48	40	Hollow (Rev. R. Phillips, 1895).
	,,	(B)	18	17·9	15	44	37	
Box Hill	,,	(A)	11·2	13·4	...	...	...	1890 (J. L.).
(Burford Br.)	,,	(B)	12·4	...	...	...	...	,, ,,
	,,	(C)	11·6	13·4	...	...	...	,, ,,
*Birchingrove Farm	,,		8	12·3	...	...	...	1887 (J. L.).
Mickleham Downs	,,		...	18	...	...	...	Could not be accurately measured, being surrounded by a seat (J. L.).
*Tandridge	,,		...	at 2 ft. 30·4	...	...	80	Consists of three trunks united at the base).
Warlingham	,,	(A)	17	20	...	25	51	Hollow (Rev. F. R. Marriot, 1895).
	,,	(B)	15	17	6			

Place.	County.	Girth at ground level.	Girth at 3 feet.	Length of Bole.	Height.	Diameter of umbrage.	Remarks.
		Feet.	Feet.	Feet.	Feet.	Feet.	
Ashstead	Surrey	18	...	...	...	...	Original trunk dead, 1892 (J. L.).
*Cherkley Court	,, (A)	11	15	...	24	...	1890 (J. L.).
	,, (B)	13·8	23·4	...	32	...	,, ,,
	,, (C)	13·7	19·11	...	...	...	,, ,,
*Norbury Park	,, (A)	13·4	16·4	...	...	...	
	,, (B)	7	11	...	...	...	Top broken at 10 ft.; many laterals.
	,, (C)	...	11				
	,, (D)	...	14	...	...	...	Cluster of stems coalescing at 6 ft.
	,, (E)	...	18				
	,, (F)	17·3	22	Lower broken; upper 40 ft.	one	81	Druids' Grove near path; two trunks united at 5 ft.; hollow; much spray.
	,, (G)	...	18	...	25	...	Three distinct trunks from same base; below path.
	,, (H)	16·6	18	...	...	...	Surrounded by a group of stems. Below house, near station.
Addington	,,	15	17	7	40	38	'Hollow, and surrounded by young growth' (Rev. A. Carr, 1895).
Titsey Place, near Godstone	,,	at 5 ft. 18·6	...	...	48	68 70	1838 (Loudon).
*Crowhurst	,,	...	at 4 ft. 30·9	...	...	...	1850 (Brailey).
	,,	...	31	...	...	...	1877 (Jennings).
	,,	...	31·8	...	...	...	1890 (J. L.).
Brooke House, Lindfield	Sussex (1)	...	15	} ...	...	...	1896 (Mrs. S. Clarke).
	,, (2)	...	10				
	,, (3)	...	10·4				
*Hardham	,,	21 ft. in 1835	...	...	...	...	Horsfield's *Sussex*. Destroyed by storm, 1846 (Rev. J. M. Sandham).
Woolbeding	,,	12	14	7	45	48	'Hollow; trunk has a gap of 18 inches on one side, and is surrounded by young shoots' (Rev. E. L. Elwes).
Cold Waltham	,,	...	31·3	6	39·2	64	Hollow; much spray (Rev. W. H. Starling).
Buxted	,,	33	39	6	55	60	'Trunk sound'l Cavity where branches start; twelve years ago lost three large branches from weight of snow (Rev. J. P. Gell). 'A noble old yew-tree, measuring 23·4 in circumference' (Sussex Arch. Coll.).

Place.	County.	Girth at ground level.	Girth at 3 feet.	Length of Bole.	Height.	Diameter of umbrage.	Remarks.
		Feet.	Feet.	Feet.	Feet.	Feet.	
*Crowhurst	Sussex	...	26·9				
Gravetye (Mill Place Farm)	,,	...	at 5 ft. 10·6	...	...	...	W. Robinson, Esq.
Etchingham	,,	...	18	...	...	...	'Much broken by storms,' 1895 (Rev. A. R. Lamplugh).
Icklesham	,,	19	15·6	...	45	57	1895, 'hollow, but still healthy' (Rev. T. T. Churton).
Hurstmonceaux	,,	...	30	...	...	...	Surrounded by young spray, 1894 (J. L.).
Wilmington	,,	22	at 2 ft. 22	2	56·9	69	At 2 ft. divides into two limbs, S. 13·10 in girth, N. 14·9.
Kinglye Vale (near hut)	,, (1)	...	13·9				A group of many hundred trees, some of large size, 1895 (J. L.).
	,, (2)	...	11				
	,, (3)	...	11·5	...	...	...	
(end of road on hill)	,, (4)	...	15·4				
	,, (5)	...	15				
E. Lavant	,,	at 18 in. ...	16·1	...	...	...	Hollow, central root, four large branches, 1895.
Stedham	,,	28·6	...	...	...	...	Hollow, *Gard. Chron.*, May 1, 1880.
Cowdray	,,	...	16	...	30	...	1838 (Loudon).
Studley Park	Warwickshire	...	14·3	...	...	...	1838 (Loudon).
Yewdale	Westmoreland	...	26·2 at 2 ft.	25	...	...	Dr. Christison.
*Lorton	,,	...	23·10	...	...	...	Professor Knight.
*Patterdale	,,	...	16	...	...	...	'Blown down in 1833' (Rev. G. B. R. Hale).
Longleat	Wilts	...	31	(?)	...	...	'Said to be 300 years old'! (Loudon, 1838).
Tisbury	,, (A)	...	37	...	...	...	Sir T. Dick Lauder, 1834. 'Hollow; nine persons can stand inside; young shoots from trunk.'
*Tytherley	,, (B) Wilts	31 10·6	30·6 ...	... ...	... ...	... 50	Rev. H. Morland, 1892. 1838 (Loudon).
Stanton	Worcester	25	at 5 ft.	...	...	...	Lees, *Gard. Chron.*, 1874.
Kyre Park	,, (A)	30	24	12	40	...	Split in two, 1895 (Mrs. Baldwyn-Childe).
	,, (B)	36	32	20	50	65	

Place.	County.	Girth at ground level.	Girth at 3 feet.	Length of Bole.	Height.	Diameter of umbrage.	Remarks.
		Feet.	Feet.	Feet.	Feet.	Feet.	
Kyre Park (Woodpatch Grove)	Worcester	30	26	...	...	63	Split in two, 1895 (Mrs. Baldwyn-Childe).
Backleton Churchyard	,,	...	at 4 ft. 21	...	...	...	1838 (Loudon).
Tardebigge	,,	15·8	18·6				
Aldby Park	Yorkshire	...	10 9·4	...	...	...	Both compound trees formed by union of two distinct trunks. They are evidently not 200 years old. House built 1726. Not infested with galls.
*Fountain's Abbey	,, (1)	13		...	...	...	Evelyn, 1770, on the hills. For further details, v. p. 212.
	,, (2)	18					
	,, (3)	19					
	,, (4)	21					
	,, (5)	25					
	,, (6)	26·6					
	at (7)	3 ft. 6 in. 18·6	at 7 ft. 25·3	...	...		Near the Abbey (Rev. Mr. Bittleson, 1880). Christison.
	,,	...	20·10 at 5 ft. 22·6				Measured by myself in 1891.
Spotborough Hall, Doncaster	,,	...	15·6	...	34	63	1838 (Loudon).

In Scotland

'YEW-TREES IN SCOTLAND' OF 10 FEET IN GIRTH AND UPWARDS

(*Chiefly taken from Mr. Hutchison's Paper*)

Place.	County.	Girth at 1 foot.	Girth at 2 feet.	Girth at 3 feet.	Length of Bole.	Height.	Diameter of umbrage.	Remarks.
		Feet.	Feet.	Feet.	Feet.	Feet.	Feet.	
Ellon Castle	Aberdeen	...	12	...	...	27	24	
,,		...	13	...	...	30	18	
,,		...	11	...	...	30	18	
,,		...	10·9	...	...	32	23	
,,		12	...	...	...	27	15	
,,		12	...	...	...	20	14	
,,		...	12	...	...	20	14	
,,		...	10·6	...	...	18	14	
,,		...	10·8	...	...	18	14	
,,		...	10·6	...	...	18	22	
,,		...	14	...	...	25	22	
,,		...	11	...	...	27	22	
,,		...	...	14	...	24	24	
,,		...	...	...	6	28	28	'Measured 10·6 at 1 foot in 1852.'
Pitmedden	,,	9·7	...	...	10·8	...	...	Planted by Sir A. Seton in 1675.
	,,	14·6	...	14	...	25	41	
	,,	13·9	...	13	...	28	45	
Old Meldrum Manse	,,	10	...	...	12	27·6	...	
	,,	10·2	...	...	12	28		
	,,	11·2	9					
*Loudon Castle	Ayrshire	13·8	...	13·10	6	44	74	
	,,	11·7	...	10·5	12	40	...	'Taken from a growth of twenty-nine south of the Castle.'
	,,	10·4	...	9·6	10	40		
Cloncaird Castle	,,	...	12·2	...	6	40	61	
*Dryburgh	Berwick	14·3	11·4	11·4	7·10	...	...	'In June 1863 it was 6·11 at 8 ft. up, and not much above 20 ft. high.'
Bonhill	Dumbarton	...	11·2	...	8	32		
Rossdhu (Luss)	,,	...	12·7	...	...	36		
	,,	...	13·3	12·8	...	52		
*Inch Lonaig	,, (A)	...	13	...	10	35	...	'Has been eaten bare nearly all round by wild goats. Now recovering.'
	,, (B)	...	10·7					
*Roseneath	,,	15·0	...	11·2	13	50	57	

* Those marked thus * are referred to in chap. xii.

Place.	County.	Girth at 1 foot.	Girth at 2 feet.	Girth at 3 feet.	Length of Bole.	Height.	Diameter of umbrage.	Remarks.
		Feet.	Feet.	Feet. at 6 ft.	Feet.	Feet.	Feet.	
Forgan, St. Andrews	Fife	...	...	12·5	18	...	...	'Popular tradition (!) as to the age of the group places them as at least 600 years old.'
Kirton of Forgan	,,	14	...	12·5	4	...	66	
Glamis Castle	Forfar	10·3	...	11·6	8	32	45	'Many others of similar dimensions.'
*Ormiston Hall	Haddington	13·10	15·0	19·8	10 at 5 ft.	35	217 circ.	'An historical tree' (Hutchison).
	,,	12·9	13·6	14·9	17·8	...	58	In 1834 (Loudon).
Whittinghame	,,	11·4	...	10·8	10	45	106	,, ,,
Yester	,,	10·4	12·8	,...	...	30		
Glenmorriston, Fort Augustus	Inverness	...	14	...	...	...	80	Christison.
Old Castle	Kincardine	13·6	...	...	...	45	...	1836 (Loudon).
Cleish Castle	Kinross	12	...	...	...	...	...	'Forty trees from 7 ft. to 12 ft. in girth.'
Craignethan Castle	Lanark	10·5	...	...	10	42		
Rosslyn	Midlothian	10·3	...	8·9	12	42·8	...	The Rev. J. Munn, 1896.
Hatton House	,,	10·6	9·9	... at 5 ft.	...	50	45	
Abercairny	Perth	...	...	10·7	6	35	...	'At one time sheltered the Marquis of Montrose.'
Lawers	,,	10·4	...	12·6	8	37·8	46	
	,,	14·4	...	...	None	32·8	60	'Branches into spreading head near the ground.'
*Fortingal	,,	56	...	...	...	...	...	1771 (Hon. Daines Barrington).
Parkhill Blairgowrie	,,	14·5	...	15 at 5 ft.	7	26	...	'Shaped like a mushroom, was probably planted in 1810.'
Dargavel	Renfrew	9·4	...	12·2	14	30		
Craigends	,,	21	...	...	1·6	41·9	80 yds. circ.	'Breaks at 2 ft. into fourteen limbs of upright growth, and from 9 ft. at 3 ft. in girth.'
Ferniehurst Castle	Roxburgh	...	10·7	... at 5 ft.	...	...	...	'Supposed to be 500 years old.'
Ballikinrain	Stirling	11·5	...	11·8	...	48·8	67	
Bantaskine	,,	11	..	12·4	7	40	70	
Callander Park	,,	11·0	...	...	...	...	...	1836 (Loudon).
Arngomery	,,	15·6	...	10·4	7·6	36	67	'Old buildings, taken down lately near site, were of eleventh century.'

YEW-TREES OF 10 FEET IN GIRTH AND UPWARDS IN IRELAND

Place.	County.	Girth at ground level.	Girth at 3 feet.	Length of Bole.	Height.	Diameter of umbrage.	Remarks.
		Feet.	Feet.	Feet.	Feet.	Feet.	
Killyleigh Castle In 1st garden	Down . (A)	...	at 2 ft. 12	12	35	64	*T. Hibernica.* Weeping variety; branches reach ground at 15 feet, forming tent.
,, and garden	,, . (B) ,, . (C) ,, . (D)	... ...	at 4 ft. 10 each 10 10	... 4 5·4	... 35 35	66 62 ...	Do. do. Roots and branches interlaced.
,, Kitchen garden	,, . (E) ,, . (F)	10 10	... ...	... ..	... 40	... ...	} Twin stems (Col. A. R. Hamilton).
Moira . .	,, .	16	...	...	45	39	Colonel Richardson.
Castle Ward, Downpatrick	,, . ,, . ,, . ,, . ,, . ,, . ,, .	11·5 10·0 10·0 11·5 11·5 11·6 10·3					There are sixty trees in lines on terraces; nineteen of them have a girth of from 8 feet to 11 feet 6 inches (Viscountess Bangor).
Loughcrew .	Dublin (A) ,, (B)	11 10·7	... ...	8·8 9·7	... ...	... ...	Part of row of 14 trees (W. Dixon, Esq.).
Clontarf .	,,	12	12·8	...	40	76	'Not hollow: no young shoots' (H. B. Leech, Esq., LL.D.).
Rossfad, Ballinamallard	Fermanagh .	13	12·6	...	42	72	
Crom Castle	,,	12	...	6	25	77	Lord Erne (*Ulster Journal of Archæology*, Oct. 1895).
*Gartnamara	Galway .	12·5	at 5 ft. 22·6	6	40	50	At 5 feet 'spreads into 20 great branches' (E. W. Lynam, Esq.).
Muckross Abbey	Kerry . . ,, . .	10 10	... ...	13 ...	...	...	Fraser.
Fornace .	Kildare .	...	at 6 ft. 12	...	...	66	Fraser's *Handbook for Ireland*, 5th Ed., 1860, p. 66.
Maynooth .	,, (A) ,, (B) ,, (C) ,, (D) ,, (E)	... ...	at 6 ft. 20 12 12 at 5 ft. 14 11·6	... ...	50 26 24 30 38	78 37 28 33 42	In College Square.

* Referred to in chap. xii.

94 Yew-Trees of Great Britain and Ireland

Place.	County.	Girth at ground level.	Girth at 3 feet.	Length of Bole.	Height.	Diameter of umbrage.	Remarks.
		Feet.	Feet.	Feet.	Feet.	Feet.	
Carton, Maynooth	Kildare (F)	...	at 2 ft. 11	...	40	65 ⎫	These form part of a group of 5 near the pergola.
	,, (G)	...	at 3 ft. 12·6	...	28	32 ⎬	
	,, (H)	...	10	...	28	... ⎭	
	,, (I)	...	at 2 ft. 10·6	4	25	24	Between pergola and boathouse (Mr. W. A. Black).
Carrigallen, Drumsilla House	Leitrim .	...	12·8	...	...	...	Capt. O'Brien.
Rockmanshull House, Jenkinstown	Louth . .	...	10	...	...	46	W. Beck, Esq.
Barmeath, C. Dunleer	,,	10	...	...	...	...	Mr. Carolan.
Millford, Hollymount	Mayo . .	10·2	...	...	...	...	Mrs. Perrin.
Rathkenny House, Slane	Meath (A)	13	⎫				
	,, (B)	12	⎪				
	,, (C)	11·6	⎬ ...	...	...	... {	D. T. in *Irish Times*, Jan. 1897.
	,, (D)	11	⎪				
	,, Four others	10	⎭				
Ballynure House, Clones	Monaghan	...	14	...	40	69	'Ballynure' means 'The Town of the Yew' (Mrs. Haire Foster).
Strokestown House	Roscommon	13 to 9 five trees	...	...	...	...	J. A. D. in *Irish Times*, Jan. 20, 1897.
Donington, Athlone	Westmeath .	14	...	...	50	...	Wellington Gray, Esq.
	,,	13·6					
	,,	11					
	,,	10·6					
Glencormack Kilmacannac	Wicklow (A)	...	17·5				
	,, (B)	...	9·10	...	...	...	Three smaller, measure 9·10, 6·11, and 9·2 feet.
	,, (C)	...	11·10				
	,, (D)	...	11·4	...	...	...	R. S. Langworth-Damer, Esq.
	,, (E)	...	12·1				
	,, (F)	...	10·5				
	,, (G)	...	10				
	,, (H)	...	11·4				
	,, (I)	...	11·4				
	,, (J)	...	10·5				
Rossanagh .	,, .	...	...				
Ashford, .	,, .	14	...	*Nil.*	60	105	'Not hollow. No young shoots' (Col. Tighe).

TREES OF 30 FEET GIRTH AND UPWARDS IN ENGLAND AND WALES

Place.	County.	At ground.	At 3 feet.
		Feet.	Feet.
Hampstead Marshall	Berks	47	...
Pantllydw	Carnarvon	30	18
Bettwys-Newydd	,,	30·6	...
Tisbury	Dorset (A)	31	30½
,, (B)	,,	...	37
St. John, Withycombe	Devon	30	Compound tree
Darley Dale	Derbyshire	27	30
Trentham	,,	33·6	17·6
Schowle	Gloucester	30	...
Dibdin	Hants	...	30
South Hayling	,,	35	38
Warblington	,,	26	30
Breamore	,,	30	...
Ulcombe	Kent	...	35·2
Harrietsham	,,	...	30
Leeds	,,	28	32·6
Ankerwyke	Middlesex	25	30·9 (35 at 7 ft.)
Llanthewy Bach	Monmouth	31	32·5
Mamhilad	,,	30·9	29·10
Goytre	,, (A)	32·4	22
	,, (B)	30·4	...
Llanfoist	,,	32	...
Church Preen	Salop	40·5	21·9
	,,	at 1 ft., 30·10	...
Hambledon	Surrey	36	39
Tandridge	Sussex	34	...
Cold Waltham	,,	...	31·3
Buxted	,,	33	39
Hurstmonceaux	,,	...	30
Kyre Park	Worcestershire	30	24
	,,	36	32
	,,	30	26

CHAPTER VII

Why planted in churchyards — Druidical, Roman, and Christian customs—Early English writers—Funeral customs—Symbolism—Shelter of buildings—For providing bow-wood—Hansard's objections—Planted in churchyards in Germany and Normandy.

THE custom of planting yew in churchyards is a very old one, as is proved by a statement of Giraldus Cambrensis, who visited Ireland in A.D. 1184, and observed it in cemeteries and holy places:—

'Prae terris autem omnibus quas intravimus, longe copiosus amaro hic succo taxus abundat, maxime vero in Cœmiteriis antiquis, locisque sacris sanctorum virorum manibus olim plantatas (al. plantatis), ad decorem et ornamentum quem addere poterant, arborum istarum copiam videas.'[1]

There are various reasons suggested to account for the frequent occurrence of yew-trees in churchyards and in the immediate vicinity of consecrated buildings, some of them having a show of reason. It may be that the statement in Ossian[2] is true, that 'The yew was a funereal tree, the companion of the grave among the Celtic tribes. Here rests

[1] *Topog. Hibern.*, dist. iii. cap. x. Ed. J. E. Dimock; London, 1867.
[2] Vol. i., 8th ed. p. 240.

YEW-TREES IN DRUIDS' GROVE, NORBURY PARK.

their dust, Cuthullin! These lonely yews sprang from their tomb and shaded them from the storm'; but there is no reliable evidence of the aboriginal tribes regarding the yew with any special veneration, and there does not appear to be any authentic instance of their planting it near the sacred circles. Several writers have entered into this question, and presume that the yew was one of those evergreens which, from its shade and shelter, was especially cultivated by the Druids in their sacred groves and around their sacrificial circles, ignoring the fact that these were always placed in situations whence the rising and setting of the sun, over some prominent feature of the landscape, could be observed at the time of sacrifice ; that when Christianity superseded Druidism the same places were chosen as the sites of the new worship ; and that in this manner arose the association of the yew-tree with our churches and churchyards. This may be so, but I have been unable to discover a single instance of a Druidical stone being associated with a church. It may also be true, as surmised by some, that it was used by the early Roman invaders in their funeral rites in lieu of their accustomed cypress and pine.[1] Of Picea, Pliny says : 'funebri indicio ad fores posita.' Sir Thomas Browne seems to have first suggested that as their 'funeral pyre consisted of sweet fuel, cypress, fir, larix, yew, and trees perpetually ver-

[1] *Hydriopathia*, ch. iv.

dant, silent expressions of their surviving hopes,' the planting of yews in churchyards may have originated from these ancient funeral rites, or as an emblem of the resurrection. The tree is held in great veneration in some parts of the N.W. Himalaya; it sometimes is called *Deodār* (God's tree); the wood is burnt for incense, branches are carried in religious processions in Kamaon, and in Nepal the houses are decorated with the green twigs at religious festivals.[1]

Mr. Charles Coote says:[2] 'But of these old-world Roman superstitions that connected with the yew-tree is the most interesting. For as of old it was connected with the passage of the soul to its new abode, so ever since the introduction of Christianity into this country it has continued to adorn the last resting-place of the body, which the soul has left.'

Statius says:[3] 'Necdum illum (in Amphiaraum) aut truncâ lustraverit obvia taxo eumenis.'

Amphiaraus had descended into Hades so abruptly that the Eumenis had no time to purify him by a touch of the holy yew branch.[4]

That the sombre and gloomy character of the leaves, and their poisonous nature, are suggestive of death, is scarcely, as has been alleged, a reason for these trees being planted in churchyards, but it is

---

[1] Brandis, *Forest Flora of India*. [2] *The Romans in Britain*, 1878.
[3] *Thebaïd* viii. 9 and 10. [4] 6 Ser. ii. 1880, p. 256.

certain that from very early times it has been used at funerals. This practice is mentioned by many early English writers; for instance, by Thomas Stanley, writing in 1651 :

> 'Yet strew
> Upon my grave
> Such offerings as you have,
> Forsaken cypresse and sad Ewe,
> For kinder flowers can take no birth
> Or growth from such unhappy Earth.'

And again, in the *Marrow of Compliments, etc.*, published in 1655 :

> 'Every hand and every head
> Bind with cypresse and sad Ewe.'

Evelyn says:[1] 'The best reason that can be given why the yew was planted in churchyards, is that branches of it were often carried in procession, on Palm Sunday, instead of Palms. In Nichol's *Extracts from Church-warden's Accounts*[2] is the following note as to the use of yew on Palm Sunday: 'A.D. 1525—paid for kaks, flowers and Yow, ii^d.'

Brady's *Clavis Calendaria*, vol. i. pp. 276-80, says that in commemoration of our Saviour's entry into Jerusalem, 'the Church has, from the earliest period, held this day in the highest respect. Among our superstitious forefathers the *palm-tree or its substitutes, box or yew*, were solemnly blessed,

[1] *Sylva*, p. 267.   [2] P. 272 (4th ed. 1797).

and some of their branches burnt to ashes and used by the priests on the Ash Wednesday of the following year, while other boughs were gathered and distributed among the pious, who bore them about in their numerous processions'—'a practice which was continued in this country until the second year of Edward VI., when it was abolished as superstitious.'[1]

The following extract from Caxton's *Direction for keeping Feasts all the Year* is decisive on this custom. In the lecture for Palm Sunday, he says: 'Wherefore Holy Chirche this day makyth solemn processyon, in memory of the processyon that Cryst made this day. But for the eucheson that we have none Olyve that bereth grene leef, algate therefore we take Ewe instead of palm and olyve, and beren about in processyon, and so is thys day called Palm Sonday.' As a confirmation of this fact it is said that the yew-trees in the churchyards[2] of East Kent are at this day called Palms, as also in Ireland, where it is still the custom for the peasants to wear in their hats or buttonholes sprigs of yew, from Palm Sunday until Easter Day,[3] and Ablett[4] says that the branches were carried over

---

[1] *Notes and Queries*, 5F. xii. 192.
[2] In the Churchwardens' account of Woodbury, Devonshire, is the following entry: 'Memorandum, 1775. That a yew- or palm-tree was planted in the churchyard, ye south side of the church, in the same place where one was blown down by the wind a few days ago, this 25th of November.'
[3] Johns, *The Forest Trees of Great Britain*.   [4] *English Trees*.

YEW AT WARBLINGTON.
From a photograph by Scorer, *Havant.*

the dead by mourners and thrown beneath the coffin in the grave. The yew being an evergreen was considered typical of the immortality of man. This was the view held by Ray the naturalist, but the idea seems in both instances to have been taken from Sir Thomas Browne.

While therefore the evergreen foliage and the enduring nature of the wood were symbolic of the immortality of the soul, the rejuvenescence so peculiar to the yew would be an emblem of the resurrection. Mr. Bowman[1] assumes that the Pagan customs in use by our ancestors would be retained and engrafted on Christianity on its first introduction.

'When Augustine was sent by Gregory the Great to preach Christianity in Britain, he was enjoined to purify and not to destroy the temples of Pagan worship; and it is not unlikely that the very presence of the venerable yews would prove an attraction to these sites. The old Pagans, like the modern heathen, loved to place trees round the place of worship.'

It should be observed that this is a mere assumption. St. Augustine's injunction had reference no doubt to Roman temples, and possibly to Druidical places of worship, so far as I know, but there is little evidence to prove that the ancient Britons held the yew in any reverence, and, as has

[1] *Magazine of Natural History*, New Series, vol. iv.

been previously remarked, their temples were always placed in open spaces, and not amongst trees.

Another reason alleged for their being planted in such localities seems to have been the very strange one of providing shelter for the sacred buildings. Thus in a Statute of Edward I. provision of this kind is made, but the Statute 35 Edward I. (A.D. 1307)[1] was merely a repetition of one embodied (A.D. 1215) in Magna Charta,[2] 'Ne Rector prosternet arbores in Cemeteris :' 'Arbores ipse propter ventorum impetus ne Ecclesiis noceant, sepe plantantur. Prohibemus, ne Ecclesiarum Rectores ipsas presumant prosternere indistincte, nisi cum Cancellus Ecclesiae necessaria indigent refectione. Nec in alios usus aliqualiter convertantur.'

This passage may possibly not have reference to the yew. Otherwise it seems to be an absurd injunction for the protection of the churches. As a writer in the *Gentleman's Magazine*[3] truly says : 'Scarce any (tree) could be selected which is so ill adapted to be planted for protection, from the slowness of its growth and the horizontal direction of its branches, both of which prevent it rising high enough, even in a century, to shelter from storms a building of moderate height.' If yew hedges

[1] *Secunda pars Veterum Statutorum*; Lond. 1556, 12mo, Signat. E. 5.
[2] Brand, *Pop. Antiq.*   [3] 1786, vol. lvi. p. 941.

were planted for this purpose it is strange that only individual trees remain.

While admitting that the above-named causes may have had some part in the planting of yew-trees in churchyards, it is pretty certain that there must have been a much more cogent reason in operation to account for the very widely extended practice which obtained throughout the country. And this was the necessity of providing a supply of bow-staves for our English bowmen, whose prowess with their favourite weapon had gained them so much distinction and done so much to advance our national greatness. Accordingly we find many enactments both for planting and protecting yew-trees. Thus there was ordered, in the reign of Richard III., 1483, a general plantation of yew-trees for the use of archers.[1] And in the reign of Elizabeth it was enjoined that they should be planted in churchyards and cemeteries, partly to ensure their cultivation and protection, and partly to secure their leaves from doing injury to cattle.

There can be no doubt that a certain amount of bow-wood was obtained in this way, but the supply could not have equalled the wants of the villagers; this is proved by the fact, which equally proves the scarcity and inferiority of English-grown bows, that whilst these sold for 3s. 4d. each,[2] foreign ones fetched 6s. 8d. And there was an enactment in

[1] Stow's *Chronicle*.   [2] Strutt, *Sylva Brit.*, p. 7.

force that a certain number of bow-staves were to be imported with every butt of wine from Venice and elsewhere.

It is not unlikely that yews may have been planted in great numbers in churchyards and other enclosures, and that only a few of these have survived the severe cutting to which they were subjected. It must not be forgotten, however, that Giraldus' statement shows that the practice was common long before any steps were taken for providing a supply of bows in this manner.

Hansard[1] gives the following reasons against their having been planted in churchyards for this purpose :—

'Is it not absurd to suppose that men would plant, within these contracted bounds, a single tree of such slow growth, that in the space of a century its height and substance are scarcely sufficient to supply half a dozen bow-staves, while numbers were courting the bowman's axe on every hill-side?'

'The piety, or, as some men choose to style it, the superstition, of our ancestors would have been decidedly opposed to the application of wood reared within consecrated ground to any such purpose.'

'Not within consecrated ground only, but even the domain of the clergy. When Henry IV. issued his commission to Nicholas Frost, the royal bowyer,

[1] G. A. Hansard, *The Book of Archery*, etc., 8vo, 1841.

to enter upon the lands of private individuals and cut down yew or any other wood for the public service, he expressly forbids his trespassing on estates belonging to any religious order.'

'Every yew-tree growing within the united churchyards of England and Wales, admitting they could have been renewed five times in the course of a century, would not have produced one-fiftieth part of the bows required for military supplies.'

On the other hand, we find that Charles VII. of France ordered it to be planted in all the churchyards of Normandy for the express purpose of providing wood for cross-bows.

Strutt says :[1] 'It was formerly not less common in the churchyards of Italy; and in the original charter for building the church at Pérone, in Picardy, dated in the year 684, a remarkable clause is inserted containing directions for the proper preservation of a particular yew-tree. This *individual yew-tree* (!) was in existence in the year 1799, nearly (*sic*) 1100 years after this notice in the charter.' There is no evidence of this being the same tree which was planted in 684. There may have been several since that date.

A curious Scottish superstition in reference to the yew as a consecrated tree is mentioned in the 'Recollections of O'Keefe' published in *Ainsworth's Magazine*, vol. iii. As related by him :—

[1] *Op. cit.* p. 1.

'It is an idea in the north of Scotland that a person, when grasping a branch of churchyard yew in his left hand, may speak to any one he pleases, but however loud he may call, the person spoken to will not be able to hear what is said, though the words will be audible to all around. O'Keefe mentioned that a man who wished to prejudice the clan against their chief without receiving punishment for his rashness, approached the chief when all his clan were around him, and bowing profoundly as if to show his devotion, with the branch of yew in his hand, spoke in the most insulting and defiant manner for all around to hear. The result of this strange experiment may easily be conceived.'[1]

Forby, in his *East Anglian Vocabulary*, says that it is a superstitious notion that—

'If you bring yew into the house at Christmas amongst the evergreens used to dress it, you will have a death in the family before the end of the year.'[2]

[1] *Notes and Queries*, 6 Ser. ii. 1880, p. 184.
[2] *Ibid.*, 1 Ser. vii. 447.

CHAPTER VIII

Character of Yew wood—Uses—Manufacture—Value—
'Saint's Yew.'

THE wood is hard, close-grained, of a deep red brown colour, and finely veined; the sapwood is yellowish white. It was formerly much used in the manufacture of Tunbridge ware. It is converted into 'cogs for mills, posts to be set in the ground, and everlasting axle-trees'; for these, says Evelyn, 'there is none to be compared with it.' Bows also are made from it, and spoons, cups, and 'flood-gates for fish-ponds, which hardly ever decay.'[1]

A remarkable property possessed by it is given on the authority of Boucher, that the wooden part of a bed made of yew 'will most certainly not be approached by bugs.' 'Cabinet-makers and inlayers (particularly for parquetry floors) most gladly employ it.'[2]

Evelyn continues: 'likewise for bodies of lutes, theorboes, bowls, wheels, and pins for pulleys; yea, and for tankards to drink out of.'[3] He denies

---

[1] Withering, *British Plants.* [2] Selby, *Brit. Forest Trees*, p. 371.
[3] Evelyn, *Sylva*, vol. i. p. 258, 1776.

Pliny's assertion, and says that the ill repute it bore for drinking-vessels had no foundation, and maintains that the toxic quality was in the liquor and not in the wood. In this he is partly right and partly wrong. No doubt, in most instances, the poison was in the liquor, but it is also true that the wood is poisonous, and it is possible that wine, especially if it had stood for some time in a new vessel, might extract sufficient poison to be injurious. Water would not extract the poison, and any noxious effect would disappear after frequent use as a wine-vessel. At the present day it is used as the favourite material for making cups, etc., in the Pyrenees.

Miss Betham Edwards writes:[1] 'These folks being great water-drinkers, will have their water in a state of great perfection. Some native genius long ago invented a vessel which answers the requirements of the most fastidious. This is a pail-shaped receptacle of yewen wood, bound with brass bands, both inner and outer parts being kept exquisitely clean. Water in such vessels remains cool throughout the hottest hours of the hottest summer, and the wood is exceedingly durable, standing wear and tear, it is said, hundreds of years. The turning and encasing of yewen wood and brass-bound water-jars is a flourishing manufacture at Osse.'

[1] *France of To-day*, 1892.

In India[1] it is used for native bedsteads, bows, jampan poles, upholstery, and clogs. 'Whip-handles are also made of the branches, and from time immemorial it has been the principal wood used for bows.'[2]

'The bark (*sang, sangha*) is exported to Ladak from Kunawar, to be mixed with tea and to be used as a red dye.'

In Ireland the wood is used for rungs of ladders. Captain O'Brien of Drumsilla House, Carrigallen, writes that he has had some in use for thirty years, and they are as sound as ever.

Loudon says:[3] 'The fineness of its grain is owing to the thinness of its annual layers, 280 of these being sometimes found in a piece not more than 20 inches in diameter.'

'The sapwood, though of as pure a white as the wood of the holly, is easily dyed of a jet black, when it has the appearance of ebony.'

In Wales, great value used to be set upon the yew-tree; as is proved by the ancient Welsh laws,[4] the consecrated yew of the priests having got to supplant in value the sacred mistletoe of the Druids. The following extract of the ancient Welsh laws fixes the value of the different trees. It must be borne in mind that at the age to which it refers, fruit-trees, such as apple-trees, were comparatively scarce.

[1] Balfour, *Trees, etc., of India*.   [2] Brandis, *Forest Flora of India*.
[3] *Arboretum*.   [4] *Cambrian Register*, vol. vi. p. 332.

'A consecrated yew, its value is a pound.
A mistletoe branch, three score pence.
An oak, six score pence.
Principal branch of an oak, thirty pence.
A yew tree (not consecrated), fifteen pence.
A sweet apple, three score pence.
A sour apple, thirty pence.
A thorn-tree, sevenpence half-penny.
Every tree after that, four pence.'[1]

Upon looking into the *Leges Wallicae*,[2] I find the following: '14. Taxus xxx denarios valet. 22. Taxus silvestris, xv denarios valet. 23. Taxus *Sancti* libram valet,' with the subsequent note: 'Sancti Sancto nempe alicui dicata, Dubritio v. gr. vel Teliao quales apud Wallos in Cemeteriis etiam-num frequenter visuntur.' So that the above ought to be translated 'A Saint's Yew is a yew dedicated to some Saint.'

The most important use of the wood is considered in the chapter on Bows.

[1] Ablett, *English Trees*, 1880, p. 154.
[2] Wotton, *Cyfreithjew* or *Leges Wallicae*, etc., fol. Lond. 1730, p. 262. 'Taxus in Legibus Hoëli legitimum pretium non habet, quoniam eo anno quo sues strumosi sunt, juxta canis statum censetur ; et eo anno quo canes sabiosi sunt, juxta statum suis censetur' (fol. 259). In sec. cclii. fol. 386, there are exceptions to the law against cutting trees in forest lands. 'Tres arbores impune exscindere licet in salta regio: 1. arbor ad contignationem Ecclesiae conficiendam ;· 2. et arbor ad hastilia in usus regios conficienda ; 3. et materia feretri.'

CHAPTER IX

Bows—Ancient use—Long-bow—Battle of Hastings—Its value in English wars—English supremacy—Various Statutes—Forest laws—Edward II.—Edward III.—Edward IV.—French archers—Statute of Henry VIII.—Elizabeth—'Act of Bowyers'—Prices—Importation of foreign bows—Act of Philip and Mary—Companies of archers—Commission of Charles I.—Bow-making—Cross-bows made of yew—Its inferiority to the long-bow.

Bows have, from the earliest times, been made of various kinds of hard and elastic wood, and we have the testimony of Homer and Virgil that the yew was one of the principal of these. There is little doubt that it was used by the Saxons for this purpose, though Meyrick says they only used it for killing birds, and in all probability the ancient Britons made their bows of it. Certainly they used it for making spears, for I have in my possession a spear of this wood, dug up from beneath the peat in the fens of Cambridgeshire, and therefore most likely 2000 or 3000 years old.

'It is supposed that war was anciently proclaimed in Britain by sending messengers in different directions through the land, each bearing a *bended bow*; and that peace was in like manner announced by a bow unstrung, and therefore straight.'[1]

[1] *Cambrian Antiquities.*

The English long-bow seems to owe its introduction to the Normans, who, chiefly by its means, won the battle of Hastings. The figures of archers in the Bayeux tapestry show them to have been armed with the long-bow. Demmin[1] says that the Norman bow was small, being only about a metre in length, while the bow used by the English archers about the thirteenth century measured two yards in length, and varied according to the height of the person who used it.

> 'Thus thou peculiar Engine of our Land!
> (Weapon of Conquest! Master of the Field!)
> Renownèd Bow! (that mad'st this Crown command
> The Towers of France, and all their powers to yield)
>   .   .   .   .   .
> Thou first didst conquer us; then raised our skill
> To vanquish others : . . .'[2]

Ruskin[3] points out that 'the blasted trunk on the left, in Turner's drawing of the spot where Harold fell at the battle of Hastings, takes, where its boughs first separate, the shape of the head of an arrow; this, which is mere fancy in itself, is *imagination*, as it supposes in the spectator an excited condition of feeling dependent on the history of the spot.'

Besides Harold, two other English kings lost their lives through the instrumentality of the bow, viz. William Rufus, in the New Forest, and Richard

---

[1] *Weapons of War.* [2] Daniel, *History of the Civil Wars*, B. 8.
[3] *Modern Painters*, vol. i. p. 192.

NORMAN ARCHERS.
From the Bayeux Tapestry.

Cœur de Lion at Limoges, or, as Grose asserts, at Chaluz in Normandy. The latter was killed by an arrow from a cross-bow, but this, Demmin shows, was made of yew, which was planted by order of Charles VII. in all the churchyards and cemeteries in Normandy, for that purpose.

From the time of the Conquest onwards, the bow became the national arm, in the use of which the English acquired more proficiency than any other nation, from whom they differed, apparently, in their mode of shooting. The Englishman, says Gilpin, 'did not keep his left hand steady, and draw his bow with his right; but keeping his right at rest upon the nerve, he pressed the whole weight of his body into the horns of his bow. Hence probably arose the phrase of *bending* a bow, and the French of *drawing* one.'[1] The command of Richard III. at the battle which was fatal to him, was, ' Draw, archers; draw your arrows to the head.'

Whether owing to their method of shooting, or to the superiority of their weapon, the English largely surpassed other nations in the use of the bow, which in their hands was worked with terrible effect. Gibbon, speaking of the dread with which the English inspired their enemies in the Crusades, says, ' At one time Richard, with seventeen knights and three hundred archers, sustained the charge of the whole Turkish and Saracen army ' (ch. lix.).

[1] *Remarks on Forest Scenery*, 1791.

And it was by means of the bow, as Bishop Lightfoot observes,[1] 'that England rose to the first position in the commonwealth of nations, and by force of arms inspired such terror, and commanded such respect throughout Europe as it has never commanded or inspired since, and in continental politics attained an influence never afterwards surpassed, and only equalled—if even then it was equalled—many centuries later in the struggle with the first Napoleon.'

Roger Ascham[2] asserts that neither the French nor even the Scots could rival the English in archery. In the battle of Falkirk, *temp*. Edward I., the bow caused terrible slaughter amongst the Scots, who are said to have lost 12,000 men, while the English loss was only 100.

Sir Walter Scott, in *Marmion*,[3] admits the inferiority of the Scottish weapon:—

> 'But, O!
> Short was the shaft and weak the bow
> To that which England bore.'

And in the deadly fight betwixt Earls Percy and Douglas, described in the Percy Ballads :—

> 'Our English archers bent their bows,
> Their hearts were good and true,
> At the first flight of arrows sent
> Full threescore Scots they slew.'

---

[1] 'England during the latter half of the Thirteenth Century.'—Lightfoot's *Historical Essays*, p. 106.
[2] *Toxophilus*.   [3] Canto v. par. v.

Value of the Bow in English Wars 115

Philip de Comines[1] styles them 'milice redoutable la fleur des archers du monde.' And in the *Chronicle of Bertrand du Guesclin*, English archers are thus commended: 'et sans les bons archers du bon pays Anglais.'[2]

The Irish do not seem to have been much acquainted with the use of the bow until the time of Edward IV., who enforced the practice amongst the English residents and their Irish servants.

In England, the general use of it is shown by a statement of Pennant,[3] 'that in 1397, Richard II. holding a parliament in a temporary building, on account of the wretched state of Westminster Hall, surrounded it with 4000 Cheshire archers, armed with tough yew bows, to ensure freedom of debate.'

Froissart[4] thus describes the prowess of the English archers at Poictiers: 'Then the battle began on all parts, and the battles of the marshals of France approached, and they set forth that they were appointed to break the array of the archers. They entered a-horseback into the way where the great hedges were on both sides set full of archers. As soon as the men of arms entered, the archers began to shoot on both sides, and did slay and hurt horses and knights, so that the horses, when they

---

[1] *Hist. de France* (tom. iii. p. 873).
[2] Meyrick, *Ancient Armour*, vol. iii. Glossary.
[3] London, 2nd ed. p. 39.   [4] *Chronicles*.

felt the sharp arrows, they would in no wise go forward, but drew aback and flung, and took on so fiercely that many of them fell on their masters, so that for press they could not rise again, in so much that the marshals' battle could never come at the prince.' And further: 'True to say, the archers did their company that day great advantage, for they shot so thick that the Frenchmen wist not on what side to take heed.'

In the narrative of the battle of Blanchetayne, or passage of the Somme, which took place just before that of Creçy, Froissart says:[1] 'The Frenchmen defended so well the passage at the issuing out of the water, that the English had much to do. The Genoese did them great trouble with their crossbows. On the other side, the archers of England shot so wholly together, that the Frenchmen were fain to give place to the Englishmen.'

The battle of Aljabarota in Portugal, which was fought between the kings of Portugal and Spain, the former being assisted by John of Gaunt with an English force, while the king of Spain was aided by volunteers from France and Béarn, is thus described by Froissart:—

'The same Saturday was a fair day, and the sun was turned towards evensong. Then the first battle came before Aljabarota, when the king of Portugal and his men were ready to receive them. Of these

[1] *Chronicles*, 149.

French knights there were two thousand spears, as fresh and well-ordered men as could be devised; and as soon as they saw their enemies, they joined together like men of war, and approached in good order until they came within a bow-shot; and at their first coming there was a hard encounter, for such as desired to assail, to win grace and praise, entered into the straight way, where the Englishmen by their policy had fortified them. And because the entry was so narrow, there was great press and great mischief to the assailants; for such English archers as were there, shot so wholly together that their arrows pierced men and horses, and when the horses were full of arrows they fell upon one another. . . . There were many of the lords and knights of France and Béarn taken and slain. . . .'

In besieging a fortress, bows and arrows were used from a wooden tower called a *berfreid*, *beffroi*, or *belfry*, which was brought near to the walls. Froissart thus describes one:[1] 'The English had constructed two large towers of great beams of wood, three stories high; each tower was placed on wheels, and covered over with prepared leather, to shelter those within from fire and from the arrows; in each story were one hundred archers.'

Among the records in the Tower of London,[2]

---

[1] Vol. i. c. 108; Meyrick, vol. i. p. 76.
[2] Rot. Walliae in Turr. Lond. m. 10 *in dorso*.

says Meyrick,[1] is a roll of expenses of King Edward I. at Rhuddlan Castle, in North Wales, in the tenth and eleventh years of his reign. These prove that he has mounted archers, *sagittarii*, as well as archers on foot.

The following extracts show the rate of pay for each kind: 'Thursday, 27th of August, paid to Robt. Giffard, for the wages of eight constables of cavalry, each receiving per diem 12d., and of eight hundred and fifty-seven archers, each receiving by the day 2d., and of their forty-three captains of twenties, each receiving 4d. per diem, from Tuesday the 25th day of August, for the seven following days, £55, 6s. 0d.

'Archers on Foot.

'To Master R. Giffard, for the wages of six archers, newly come, from Friday, 28th day of August, for the six following days, £0, 6s. 0d.'

Since bows were of so great value in warfare, it is not strange that English kings should have made strenuous efforts to plant and protect yew-trees, and to encourage the use of bows, by various edicts and Acts of Parliament, which also regulated their price, making provision for their importation, and forbidding their exportation.

'As far back as the thirteenth century, every person not having a greater revenue than one

[1] *Ancient Armour*, p. 135.

Statute of Edward II.

hundred pence was obligated to have in his possession a bow and arrows, with other arms offensive and defensive; and all such as had no possessions, but could afford to purchase arms, were commanded to have a bow with sharp arrows, if they dwelt without the royal forests,[1] and a bow with round-headed arrows, if they dwelt within the forests.'[2]

The words of the Statute (*temp.* Edw. II. apud Winton) are 'Ark et setes hors de foreste et en foreste ark et piles.' The latter were used to prevent the owners killing the King's deer.[3]

It was also ordained by the forementioned Statute that proper officers should be appointed to see that these weapons were kept in good order, and ready for immediate service.

In an epistle to the sheriffs of London, dated

---

[1] ' A Forrest is a certen *Territorie of wooddy grounds and fruitful pastures*, priviledged for wild beasts and foules, of Forrest, Chase, and Warren, to rest and abide in, in the safe protection of the King, for his princely delight and pleasure, which Territorie of Ground, so priviledged, is meered and bounded with unremoveable markes, meeres, and boundaries, either known by matter of record, or else by prescription: And also replenished with wilde beasts of Venerie or Chase, and with great coverts of vert, for the succour of the said wilde beastes to have their abode in: For the preservation and continuance of which said place, together with the *Vert and Venison*, there are certen particular Lawes, priviledges and Officers, belonging to the same, meete for that purpose, that are only proper unto a Forrest and not to any other place.'
—*A Treatise and Discourse of the Lawes of the Forrest*: John Manwood, Lond. 1598, p. 143.

[2] Strutt, *Sports and Pastimes*, p. 54.

[3] One of the duties of a forester in former times was to see that no unauthorised person carried bows and arrows of a kind which might be used for killing deer: 'if he find any man in the forest with bows and arrows, or with greyhounds, intending to offend there, he may arrest and imprison him, as if he had actually done the fact.'—Manwood, *op. cit.*

12th June 1349, Edward III. sets forth how 'the people of our realm, as well of good quality as mean, have commonly in their sports before these times exercised their skill of shooting arrows; whence it is well known that honour and profit have accrued to our whole realm, and to us, by the help of God, no small assistance in our warlike acts.'

Now, however, 'the said skill being laid aside, as it were wholly,' the King proceeds to command the sheriffs to make public proclamation that 'every one of the said city, strong in body, at leisure times on holidays, use in their recreations bows and arrows or piles,[1] and bolts, and learn and exercise the art of shooting, forbidding all and singular, on our behalf, that they do not after any manner apply themselves to the throwing of stones, wood, or iron, hand-ball, foot-ball, bandy-ball, cambuck, or cock-fighting, nor such-like vain plays, which have no profit in them.'

In the reign of Richard II. an Act was passed to compel all servants to shoot with them on Sundays and holidays.[2]

'Edward III., in the fifteenth year of his reign, issued an order to the sheriffs of most of the English counties, to provide 500 white bows, and

---

[1] The words of the letter are: 'Arcubus et sagittis vel pilettis aut boltis.' In the thirty-ninth year of this reign, A.D. 1349, the penalty incurred by offenders was imprisonment during the King's pleasure.—Manwood, *op. cit.*

[2] *Forest and Forest Trees*, Ingram and Co.

500 bundles of arrows for the intended war against France in 1341.'[1]

'In the fifth year of Edward IV., ch. iv. (Irish), it was enacted by Statute that 'every Englishman, and every Irishman dwelling with Englishmen, should have a bow of his own height, made either of yew, wych-hazel, ash, or anolune laburnum.'[2] The Act directs that butts should be erected in every township, which the inhabitants were to shoot at up and down, upon all feast days, under the penalty of one halfpenny for every time they omitted to perform this exercise.

A petition from the Commons to Edward IV. states that 'such bowstaffes as be brought within this Realm, be sett now to outrageous prices,' and prays that for every tun-tight of merchandise as shall be conveyed in every 'Carik, Calee, or shipp, iiii bowestaffes be brought, upon pain of forfeiture to your Highness, for lacke of bringing every such bowstaff vi s. viii d.'; and an Act of 12 Edward IV.[3] is enacted to this effect, ordering also that no bowyer might sell a bow to any of the King's subjects for more than 3s. 4d. And an Act of Richard III., A.D. 1483,[4] orders a general planting

---

[1] Hargrave, *Anecdotes*, p. 39.   [2] Strutt, *Sports*, etc.
[3] This was confirmed in the third year of Henry VII., and in the thirty-third year of his son Henry VIII.; but these Acts were repealed in the third year of Queen Mary, and the following prices were settled by Parliament; for a bow made of the best foreign wood, six shillings and eightpence: for an inferior sort, three shillings and fourpence; and for one made of English yew, two shillings.   [4] Stow.

of yew, and makes it compulsory that the bow-staves shall be brought with every butt of malmsey. In the 38th Henry VIII. the price of a yew bow for any persons between the ages of seven and fourteen years was not to exceed 12d. Bishop Latimer, in his sermon before Edward VI., tells how he learnt to bend his bow: 'In my tyme, my poore father, was as diligent to teach me to shote, as to learne any other thynge, and so I thynke other menne dyd theyr children. He taught me how to drawe, how to laye my bodye in my bowe, and not to drawe with strength of armes as other nacions do, but with strength of the bodye. I had my bowes boughte me accordyng to my age and strength as I encreased in them, so my bowes were made bigger, and bigger, for men shal neuer shot well, except they be broughte up in it. It is a goodly art, a holsome kynde of exercise, and much commended in phisike.'[1] Elizabeth put in execution the Act of Edward IV.

The words of the preamble venting the great benefits to this country arising from archery are remarkable: 'Item que come en le temps dels nobles progenitours del roy, et aussi en le temps del victorieux seigneur le roy q'ore est, ses subgetz deurs chescun part cestuy royaume ount occupez et usez sagitture ove leurs arkes.' The French,

---

[1] Latimer's Seven Sermons, preached before Edward VI., April 12, A.D. 1549.

having experienced the great superiority of the English archers, Charles VII. began likewise to encourage this exercise, and ordered the yew to be planted in all the churchyards of Normandy. 'In a short time,' says Juvenal des Ursins, a French historian, who wrote a little later than the battle of Poitiers, 'the French archers became so expert in the use of the bow, that they were able to discharge their arrows with a more sure aim than the English; and, indeed, if these archers had formed a close confederacy amongst themselves, they might have become a more powerful body than the princes and nobles of France; and, accordingly, it was the apprehension of such a result as this which caused the French king to suppress the archer army.'[1] Barrington[2] remarks that 'it seems very singular that all the laws for the encouragement of archery should be after the invention of gunpowder and fire-arms.' Lord Herbert of Cherbury, who wrote so late as the reign of James I., asserts that good archers would do more execution, even at that time, than infantry armed with musketry.

'Long after the introduction of fire-arms, in the fourteenth century, the bow continued to be the principal weapon of defence, being used both at Agincourt and Flodden Field.'[3]

[1] Lacombe, *Boutell*, p. 133.
[2] Barrington, *Observations*, 424 ; 22 Edward IV., A.D. 1482.
[3] Ablett, p. 152.

In the time of Henry VIII. archery practice had fallen so much into disuse that an Act was passed, 1511, providing, among other matters, 'that the Statute of Winchester for archery be put in due execution; and over that, that every man, being the King's subject, etc. etc., not lame, decrepit, or maimed, do use and exercise shooting with longbows, and also do have a bow and arrows ready continually in his home, to use himself in shooting.' He was also to provide bows, etc., for every manchild in his home, from seven years upwards.[1] If a servant, the cost of these might be deducted from his wages. For every infraction of this Statute the penalty was 6s. 8d.

A Statute of Philip and Mary decrees that 'all temporal persons, having estates of a thousand pounds and upwards, shall, from the 1st May 1588 (besides horses and various armour enumerated), keep "thirty bows, thirty sheaf of arrows," and so on in decreasing amounts. "Temporal persons" having 5£ and under 10£ "one long bow, one sheaf of arrowes, and one steel cap or scull," "and every person who by the Act of King Henry VIII. capt. 5," was bound by reason of certain qualifications to provide horses, armour, etc., and shall "from the 1st of May, for three months, lack or want such provision," shall forfeit "for every horse in which he is deficient, ten

[1] Hannett, *The Forest of Arden*.

pounds . . ., and for every bowe and sheaf of arrows, etc., ten shillings." One half of these penalties went to the King and Queen, the other half to the parties suing for the same.'[1]

Even so late a Statute as the 8th of Elizabeth,[2] an 'Act of Bowyers' provides that every bowyer shall have in his house fifty bows made of elm, witch-hazel, or ash, thus showing the amount of destruction which the favourite yew had undergone.

The last Statute that appears respecting the use of yew for bows is the 13th Elizabeth, cap. 14, which directs that bow-staves shall be imported into England from the Hanse towns and other places. In the above-named Act of Elizabeth the price of bows is fixed: 'Bows meet for men's shooting, being *outlandish Yew of the best sort*, not over the price of 6/8; bows meet for men's shooting of the second sort, 3/4; bows for men, of a coarser sort, called livery bows, 2/0; *bows being English Yew,* 2/0.'

Yew at length became so scarce, that to prevent a too great consumption of it, bowyers were directed to have four bows of witch-hazel or elm to one of yew. And no person under seventeen, unless possessed of moveables worth forty marks, or the son of parents having an estate of ten pounds per annum, might shoot 'in a yew bow.'[3]

[1] Grose, pp. 316, 319.   [2] Cap. x. p. 7.
[3] Grose, *Milit. Antiq.*, v. i. p. 142.

126 *Yew-Trees of Great Britain and Ireland*

In the seventeenth century, Evelyn says:[1] 'Since the use of bows is laid aside amongst us, the pro-

ENGLISH 'DOUBLE-ARMED MAN,' 1625.
From GROSE's *Military Antiquities.*

pagation of the eugh is likewise quite forborn, but

[1] *Sylva.*

the neglect of it is to be deplored.' The decline in archery had, at various times, been met by the formation of societies for its practice; thus in Wood's *Bowman's Glory*[1] we find a full account of the ceremonies in practice at the archery meetings at Mile End, instituted by Prince Arthur in the reign of Henry VII., and afterwards held by Henry VIII.

There was created in jest a Duke of Shoreditch, who was the best archer; the second and third were created Marquesses of Clerkenwell and Islington.

The Archers of the Fraternity of St. George, established by Henry VIII. in 1537, are now extinct, but their society was incorporated with the Archers' division, and, until recently, formed a branch of the Hon. Artillery Company of London.[2]

The Woodmen of Arden, the Kentish Bowmen, and the Toxophilites are still existing companies.[3]

The Royal Company of Archers in Scotland is said to have arisen in the time of James I. The Commissioners appointed by him to superintend the exercise of archery in different districts selected the most expert archers, and formed them into a company which acted as the King's principal bodyguard.[4] In the year 1703 they obtained a Royal

---

[1] *The Bowman's Glory, or Archery Revived.*
[2] Hargrave, *Anecdotes of Archery*, p. 54.
[3] *Pop. Encycl.*, Blackie.   [4] *Ibid.*

Charter from Queen Anne, confirming and multiplying their privileges.

Stow[1] shows how the enclosing of open spaces led to the disuse of archery:—

'In the east end of Fore Street is More Lane; then next is Grub Street, of late years inhabited, for the most part, by bowyers, fletchers, bowstring makers, and such-like occupations, now little occupied; archery giving place to a number of bowling-alleys and dining-houses, which in all places are increased and too much frequented.'

'What should I speak of the ancient daily exercises in the long-bow by citizens of this City, now almost clean left off and forsaken? I overpass it; for by the mean of closing in the common grounds, our archers, for want of room to shoot abroad, creep into bowling-alleys and ordinary dining-houses, near home, where they have room enought to hazard their money at unlawful games.'

Charles I. in the fourth year of his reign granted a commission under the Great Seal for enforcing the use of the long-bow.

A portion of the Royal Army, at the commencement of the Civil War, were armed with bows. The last occasion of their being used was at the siege of Devizes, under Cromwell.[2]

This was due to a deficient supply of suitable arms, and not to the superiority of bows over

[1] *Survey of London*, 1598.   [2] *Verney Memoirs*.

musketry, with their greater length of range. It is, however, singular that the bows should have been held in such esteem for so long a period after the introduction of gunpowder. No doubt in its early period the musket was an unwieldy weapon, requiring to be fired from a rest, and taking much time to load, while the bow was much more handy, and could be discharged more rapidly. Camden says:[1] 'Among the English artillery, archery challengeth the pre-eminence as peculiar to our nation'; and Alleyne (Henry VII.)—

> 'The white faith of hist'ry cannot show
> That e'er the musket yet could beat the bow.'

An archer's equipment is thus given by Chaucer[2] in his description of the 'squyers yeomen':—

> 'He was clade in cote and hode of grene,
> A shefe of peacock arrowes bright and shene
> Under his belt he bare full thriftely.
> Well coude he dresse his takel yewmanly;
> His arrowes drouped not with fethers lowe,
> And in hande he bare a mighty bowe.'

And again, in an old ballad of Robin Hood, which says of him and his followers—

> 'With them they had a hundred bowes,
> The strings were well ydight;
> An hundred shefe of arrows good,
> With hedes burnish'd full bryght;

[1] *Britannia*.   [2] *Canterbury Tales*, Prologue.

And every arrow an ell longe,
With peacoke well ydight,
And nocked they were with white silk,
It was a semely sight.'

The maker of bows was termed a 'bowyer'; of arrows a 'fletcher' (*flêche*). The frequent occurrence of these as surnames shows how prevalent such occupations were at one time in England.

In 1570 the art of bow-making had so much declined that the bowyers and fletchers petitioned Queen Elizabeth to enforce the Statute of Henry VIII. Grounds were marked out, and batteries erected, and the people enjoined to practise at Newington Butts.

Bows were rubbed with wax, resin, and tallow, and covered with waxcloth to resist the effects of damp, heat, and frost. Each bow was supplied with three good hempen strings well whipped with fine thread.'[1]

One of the rules laid down by the founder of Harrow School in 1592 ordained that the implements of archery should be supplied by the parents of every boy entering the school. 'You shall allow your child,' it said, 'at all times, bow-shafts, bow-strings, and a bracer.'[2]

An order in the Common Council Book of Chester, directs: 'For the avoiding of idleness,

---

[1] Chambers's *Book of Days*, vol. i. p. 777 (1864).
[2] *Ibid.*, vol. ii. p. 177.

all children of six years old and upwards shall, on week-days, be set to school, or some virtuous labour, whereby they may hereafter get an honest living; and on Sundays and holidays they shall resort to their parish churches, and there abide during the time of divine service, and in the afternoon all the said male children shall be exercised in shooting with bows and arrows, for pins and points only; and that their parents furnish.'

The best bows appear to have been made of Spanish yew. Thus Drayton says:[1] 'All made of Spanish yew, their bows were wondrous strong.'

Roger Ascham,[2] in his curious and amusing treatise, published in 1545, tells us that 'every bowe is made of the boughe; the plante or the boole of the tree. The boughe commonly is verye knotty, and full of prinnes weak of small pithe;... the plante is quick enough of caste, it will plye and bow far afore it breakes, and the boole is best.' He previously gives the following directions how to select a bow: 'If you come into a shoppe and fynde a bowe that is small, long, heavie and stronge, lying streighte, not wyndynge nor marred with knottes, gaule, wyndeshake, wen, freat or pynch, bye that bowe on my warrant.' And he continues: 'As for brasell, elme, wyche, and ashe, experience doth prove them to be mean for bowes; and so to conclude, ewe of all other things is that

[1] *Polyolbion*, Song 26.   [2] *Toxophilus*, p. 113.

whereof perfite shootinge would have a bowe made.'

The common yew is no longer found either in England or Europe generally, sufficiently free from knots to be useful for making bows, which are now mostly made of hickory or other American woods. Loudon suggests that if yews were planted thickly, so as to draw up the stem to a height of 8 or 10 feet, and cut down when 6 inches or 8 inches in diameter, they might still afford wood for bows. They were, in all probability, planted in this manner in former times.

The cross-bow seems to date from very ancient times; though Demmin[1] appears to think otherwise. He writes that M. Rodios supposes it to have been identical with the *gastrafetes* of the Greeks, but adds, it 'seemed to me to have been an invention of Central Europe, and to date no further back than the tenth century at earliest; for if it had been known elsewhere, the Princess Anna Comnena (1083-1148) could scarcely have been ignorant of it, inasmuch as M. Rodios gathers his information from Byzantine MSS. The Princess states, however, "the *tzagara* is a bow unknown among us."'

The only other weapon with which we are here concerned is the Norman cross-bow, which had come into favour, and was made of yew.[2] As has

---

[1] *Weapons of War*, pp. 55-57.   [2] *Op. cit.*

been said, the yew was largely planted by order of Charles VII. in Normandy for the purpose of supplying wood for the manufacture of cross-bows; and these continued in use in England till the end of the reign of Elizabeth; but it is probable that the use of yew was superseded at an early date by that of steel, which had long been employed in Italy.

It is certain that the long-bow was a more favourite weapon with the English, for the reasons which are given by Demmin.

The cross-bow, more difficult to bend, necessarily took more time. The cross-bowman could only shoot three bolts during the time in which a skilful archer might discharge from ten to twelve arrows. Besides this, rain slackened the string of the cross-bow, thereby taking away all strength; but the string of the long-bow was easily protected from damp. The loss of the battle of Creçy (1346) was partly the result of this accident, for the French bowmen could hardly make any return to the arrows of the English archers; and in 1356, when, after the defeat of Poictiers, the inferiority of the cross-bow in this respect was again shown, bodies of French archers were formed, who soon acquired so great skill as to excite the envy of the nobles, by whom they were dissolved.'

'After the defeat at Poictiers, the inferiority of the cross-bow was so evident, that in France corps of archers were formed, who soon became so expert that the nobility became fearful of their power, and they were disbanded. About 1444, besides the *gens d'armes*, the French army had twice the number of archers, and these played the same part as the mounted infantry of the present time,[1] each two having two horses, one for service, the other for baggage; "mais les deux archers n'avoient d'appointement, qu'autant qu'un homme d'armes."' The most capable and active young men of the villages were trained to the use of the bow and arbaliste, and, because of certain privileges (exempt *de la taille*), were named 'Francs Archers.' The bodies of horse and foot archers were maintained for a long period, the royal regiments under Louis XIII. (1514) being the last body of archers in France.

In obedience to a decree of the Lateran Council in 1139, which was afterwards confirmed by Pope Innocent III. the use of the cross-bow was laid aside.[2] It was re-introduced by Richard I., who was slain by a bolt or quarrel from one of these weapons, and this was considered to be a judgment on him for disobeying the injunction. Guillame le Breton,[3] relating the death of this king, puts into the mouth of Atropos, one of the Parcae, the following lines :—

[1] Fauchet, *Œuvres*, p. 527.
[2] Grose, p. 304.   [3] *Ibid.*

The Cross-bow

'Haec volo, non alia Richardum perire,
Ut qui Franci genis ballistae primitur usum.
Tradidit, ipse sui rem primus experiatur,
Quamquam alios domit, in se vim sentiat artis.'[1]

[1] *Philipid.* L. v.

YEW-TREE IN WILMINGTON CHURCHYARD.

CHAPTER X

Poisonous properties of the yew—Classical notices—Wood—Leaves—Fruit poisonous—Dangerous statements to the contrary—Effects on man—Taxin in male and female plants—Medicinal use—Valuable as a cardiac tonic—Poisonous effects on animals.

It has been well known, from very early times, that the yew possessed poisonous properties. Mention is made of this fact by Dioscorides, Nicander, Galen, and others. Caesar[1] tells us that Cativolcus, king of the Eburones, and uncle of Arminius, poisoned himself with the juice of the yew. Its use as a medicine was little known, though Suetonius tells us that the Emperor Claudian caused an edict to be published, to the effect that this tree had the marvellous power of curing the bite of vipers. Gleditsch,[2] in later times, while asserting that the tree is not poisonous, affirms that it is useful 'contre la morsure des chiens enragés.'

Plutarch makes the curious statement that it is only poisonous when in flower, as it is then always full of sap; Dioscorides says that it is especially poisonous in Italy and Gaul; while Lucretius repre-

[1] 'Rex Cativolcus, Taxo, cujus magna in Galliâ, Germania que copia est, se examinavit.'—*De Bello Gallico*, Lib. vi. xxxi.
[2] Du Hamel du Monceau, *Traité des Arbres*.

YEW AVENUE NEAR PENRHYN CASTLE.

sents it as destroying life by the odour of its flowers, a statement as erroneous as it is fanciful.

Virgil[1] alludes to the flowers as communicating poisonous properties to Corsican honey. If the yew existed in Corsica in Virgil's time, it must have been for some reason or other eradicated, for I have not met with a single tree of this species in any part of the island.

Pliny seems to have been well acquainted with its noxious properties, for he asserts that arrows were dipped in the juice to render them deadly, and that poisons were named *toxica*, formerly *taxica*, from the name of the tree *taxus*.

Statius mentions it as having poisonous properties: 'Metuendaque succo Taxus.'

Every part of the plant is more or less poisonous, with the exception of the red mucilage surrounding the ripe seeds. It is necessary to emphasise this, as so many random and careless assertions have been made on the subject. There is probably no point on which so many errors and discrepancies have arisen as on the question of the character of the *fruit*. This consists of a small nut surrounded by red fleshy pulp, and having in its interior an almond-flavoured kernel. The pulp is quite harmless in character, but it cannot be too widely known that the nut is distinctly injurious, and in large quantities poisonous. Numerous instances have

[1] *Ecl.* ix. 30.

been recorded of fatal results ensuing from having eaten the berries, which, from the sweetness of the mucilage, are very attractive to children. It is not a little strange that so many writers should have overlooked or denied their injurious character. Thus Du Hamel du Monceau :[1] 'It is said that the leaves and flowers of yew produce a poison; and that the fruit causes dysentery in those who eat them. I have, however, seen children eat them in quantity without inconvenience.'

Plutarch declares that the fruit is poisonous, and so also Pliny, who has the following: 'Gracilis et tristis, ac dira, nullo succo, ex omnibus (resiniferis) sola baccifera.' 'Mas, *noxio fructu.*' He differs from Theophrastus, who thought the fruit edible and harmless to man. Thus, he (Pliny) again writes :[2] 'Letale quippe baccis, in Hispania precipue venenum est. Hanc Sextius Smilacem a Graecis vocare dixit: et esse in Arcadiâ tam praesentis veneni, ut qui obdormiant sub ea, cibumque capiant, moviantur.'

Gerard denies the poisonous properties of the berries, 'for,' says he,[3] 'when I was yonge and went to schoole, divers of my schoole-fellows, and likewise myselfe, did eat our fils of this tree, and have not only slept under the shadow thereof, but among the branches also, without any hurt at all,

[1] *Traité des Arbres.*   [2] *Historia*, Lib. iii. cap. x. ; cap. xx.
[3] *The Herball or General Historie of Plantes*, 1636.

and that not one time but many times. . . . Daily experience showes it to be true, that the yew-tree in England is not poysonous.' Parkinson,[1] in 1629, makes a similar statement, 'and causing no harm to them for any thing that hath been knowne in our country.' 'The berries are sweet and harmless,' says Brandis, 'and are eaten by the natives of India.'[2]

Selby asserts,[3] erroneously, that the fruit does not partake of the poisonous qualities; but adds, truly enough, that the sweet mucilaginous cup surrounding the seed is quite harmless. Lindley,[4] too, writes: 'The berries are not dangerous, though the seeds are unwholesome.' But a writer in Knight's *English Encyclopædia* makes the very dangerous assertion that 'it is now well known that the fruit of the yew may be eaten with impunity.'

It is well known, on the contrary, that the fruit is very injurious, and even fatal. Taylor[5] records two cases of poisoning thus caused, one of which died comatose four hours after the berries had been eaten, and the other nineteen days afterwards, evidently from severe inflammation of the bowels. Another case is reported by Mr. Newth[6] in which death resulted from eating the berries, and two

[1] *Paradisi in Sole*, 1629.
[2] *Forest Flora of India.*
[3] *British Forest Trees.*
[4] *Vegetable Kingdom*, 231.
[5] *Medical Jurisprudence*, 10th edition.
[6] *Medical Times and Gazette*, 1870, p. 446.

are given in the *Gardener's Chronicle* for 1881. A lunatic in the Sussex County Asylum had eaten large quantities of them and was found dead. At the post-mortem examination evident signs of irritation of the stomach and intestines were discovered.

A case of poisoning by yew-berries is related by Dr. James Thompson of Droxford, Hants. The boy, aged three years, had eaten some of the berries and swallowed the stones. When first seen by the doctor he was 'just recovering from a convulsion; he was semi-comatose, but could be roused; the skin cold and clammy; breathing difficult; pupils dilated, and slight attempts at vomiting.'

Birds, such as turkeys, peacocks, and blackbirds, eat them with impunity.[1] This statement is open to doubt, but it is not unlikely that they may be able to eat a considerable quantity without injury. Blackbirds and thrushes eat a certain quantity, but from the large number of seeds found under yew-trees it would seem that they more commonly suck off the mucilage without swallowing the seeds. M. Clos,[2] of Toulouse, from a series of experiments on birds, concludes that there is much less poison in the nuts than in the leaves, and Professor Grognier,[3] of the Veterinary School of Lyons, found that 800 grammes of them administered to a fasting horse produced no ill effects, and he concluded that they were therefore not poisonous, but his experi-

[1] Ablett.   [2] Cornevin, *Plantes Vénéneuses*, p. 47.   [3] *Ibid.*

ment, as Cornevin observes, only proves that he had given an insufficient dose. Cornevin states that in Japan an oil is extracted from the seeds and used for toilet purposes.

The *wood and bark* are probably less poisonous than the leaves, but from very early times they have been held to have noxious properties. It was thought that vessels made of the wood of yew communicated their poison to the contained liquids. The quantity of poison must, however, have been small in amount, and it is not improbable, as has been suggested, that other material had been introduced. At the present day, it is said that bowls are made from this wood in the Pyrenees and used in preference to all other kinds for holding water, but then water will not dissolve the active principle of the wood as wine may do. There are as yet no exact experiments to show the amount of *taxin* which the wood contains. Cornevin's[1] researches lead him to the conclusion that the bark is poisonous, an opinion adverse to that of MM. Chevalier, Duchesne, and Reynal, who deny that it has any toxic properties. Two instances of cattle being poisoned by the bark, reported in the *Gardener's Chronicle*, December 1879, prove the accuracy of Cornevin's conclusions.

Contrary to what we find in the statements as to the fruit and wood, there seems to be no differ-

[1] Cornevin, *Plantes Vénéneuses*.

ence of opinion as to the poisonous qualities of the leaves. Evelyn's[1] assertion that the *dried* leaves produced no harmful result is perhaps the only exception, but even he shows that the *fresh* leaves, which have been given to children for the cure of worms, have caused a fatal result, and he quotes the following case in proof:—

'Dr. Percival of Manchester, in his *Medical and Philosophical Essays*, has recorded a melancholy proof of the poisonous quality of yew-leaves. "On Friday, March 25th, 1774, three children of a labouring man, near Manchester, were killed by taking a small quantity of the fresh leaves on the recommendation of an ignorant person, for the cure of worms. A spoonful of *dried* leaves was first given, followed by a drink of sour buttermilk. This produced no ill effect, and two days afterwards the same dose of *fresh* leaves was administered, causing the death of all three children. Two hours after the leaves were given they began to be uneasy; were chilly and listless; yawned much, and frequently stretched out their limbs. The eldest vomited a little, and complained of abdominal pains. The others expressed no signs of pains. No agonies accompanied their dissolution; no swelling of the abdomen ensued; and after death they had the appearance of being in a placid sleep."'

[1] *Sylva*, p. 268.

That the dried leaves are not harmless is disproved by the researches of M. Reynal,[1] which show that desiccation does not at all destroy the properties of the yew leaves, and Harmand de Mongarne[2] mentions the poisoning of a child by the powder of the leaves, administered for an attack of convulsions. Cornevin's[3] researches on the amount of poison found in the leaves at different seasons have established, he says, a curious fact: 'Contrairement à ce qui se voit pour beaucoup des phanérogames, où les parties les plus jeunes, les pousses et les feuilles encore tendres sont très veneneuses, les pousses vernales de l'if sont peu dangéreuses.'

Mr. Squarey,[4] who gives numerous instances of sheep and cows being poisoned by it, thinks that the male plant is poisonous and the female harmless to horses and cattle. Lieutenant Stuart Wortley found on analysis that but little 'taxin' exists in the female.[5] These experiments need confirmation, for there does not appear to be any physiological reason for such a difference between the sexes. The specimens examined by Lieutenant Stuart Wortley may have varied through some peculiarity of soil, but it is difficult to believe that there is so small an amount of taxin in the female as he says. If this were true the seed could not be of

---

[1] Cornevin, *Des Plantes Vénéneuses*, p. 49. [2] *Ibid.* [3] *Ibid.*
[4] *Journ. of Roy. Agricult. Soc.*, Ser. 1892. [5] *Times*, Aug. 19, 1892.

so poisonous a nature. Stuart Wortley's observations need to be confirmed.

Cases of poisoning in the human subject through taking the leaves of yew are not infrequent.

The *Lancet* quotes from *L'Imparziale* of Florence an account of a girl aged nineteen, who was advised by an old woman to drink each morning a tumblerful of a decoction of five or six ounces of the leaves. On the fourth morning the dose was increased to eight ounces. Vomiting ensued, and the patient died eight hours after taking the last dose. Mr. Balding[1] of Royston related at the Cambridge Medical Society the case of a girl who had died from the effects of yew leaves, taken for an improper purpose.

A singular case of poisoning by yew leaves is narrated by Dr. P. M. Deas.[2] A female patient in the Cheshire County Asylum was seized with an attack of faintness, followed by convulsions resembling epilepsy, and died within an hour. Five grains of yew leaves and some small seeds (? yew) were found in the stomach. She must either have chewed a larger quantity of leaves, and swallowed the juice, or some other cause of death must have existed, for five grains is far too small an amount to prove fatal in so short a time. Taylor[3] speaks of a lunatic who died in fourteen

---

[1] *British Medical Journal*, 1884, p. 818. [2] *Ibid.*, 1876.
[3] *Medical Jurisprudence.*

Medicinal use 145

hours from the effect of chewing the leaves; and another fatal case occurred in the Shrewsbury Asylum. Dr. Deas points out the dangerous consequences which may at any time result from that perversion of appetite which exists in certain cases among the insane, leading them to eat anything which comes in their way. In the presence of this tendency it would certainly seem desirable that all poisonous shrubs, and especially yew, should be excluded from the grounds of asylums.

Yew was employed as early as the seventeenth century for medicinal purposes, and Lindley[1] tells us, on the authority of an Italian physician, that yew leaves, when administered to man in small doses, have a power similar to that of digitalis over the heart and arteries, reducing the circulation, and, if persisted in too long, or given in too large doses, as certainly fatal. Dr. Schroff[2] denies that the opinion entertained by some physicians of the similarity of operation between the properties of yew and those of digitalis rests upon any physiological basis. But then he asserts that the fruit has no poisonous properties, a statement so fully disproved as to throw considerable doubt on his other allegations. I have undertaken a large series of experiments with *taxin*, made on myself at various times. The tracings of the pulse show

[1] *Vegetable Kingdom*, 231.
[2] *Zeitschrift der Gesellschaft der aerzte zu Wien*, August 1859.

beyond doubt that it is a cardiac tonic of no mean value. The heart's action is decreased in frequency by small doses, such as $\frac{1}{20}$th to $\frac{1}{8}$th of a grain, at the same time that the cardiac pressure is distinctly increased. These effects I have found to be durable. In larger doses it generally depresses the heart's action. On the whole it contrasts favourably with digitalis and convallaria, and is worthy of more extended observation.

In India, the leaves (*birmi*) are exported to the plains of the Panjab, and used medicinally as a stomachic, and in Kussawar a decoction of it is administered for rheumatism.[1]

Mr. Squarey reports[2] that two heifers were killed at Brixham, Devon, from eating the leaves of the Irish yew, and that two horses were killed in Wiltshire by a small quantity of the same variety; thus proving that the female is poisonous in a degree almost, if not altogether, equal to that of the male, for all the specimens of the Irish yew, with the one exception already noticed, are females.

Lieutenant Stuart Wortley's experiments were repeated by Professor Munro,[3] who says: 'It is quite true that in my own experiments I obtained a greater quantity of crude alkaloid in all its different stages of impurity from the male leaves than from the female; but I do not regard this result as at

---

[1] Brandis, *Forest Flora of India*.
[2] *Journ. Roy. Agricult. Soc.*, 1892.
[3] *Ibid.*

all conclusive. As at first precipitated, *taxine* is exceedingly impure, and the successive stages of purification not only reduce it very largely in quantity, but, I suspect, cause an actual alteration in composition.'

After repeated experiments he concludes that 'both male and female yew leaves contain an alkaloid. This alkaloid in both cases appears to agree with the taxine of Hilger and Brande. Taxine is probably the poison of the yew, but it is doubtful whether it has ever been obtained in a pure state, and its physiological effects have not been sufficiently studied. Other alkaloids are probably present in the yew. . . . The yew-poison may be of moderate virulence only, and may occur in greater percentage in male than in female trees, or the percentage may vary from tree to tree without distinction of sex, and this may explain the capricious occurrence of poisoning.'

The poisonous effects produced by yew on cattle and horses are very marked, and naturally of much more frequent occurrence than in the human subject. Cornevin considers that it is one of the most dangerous plants of our flora : 'Il est un de ceux qui occasionnent le plus d'accidents parce que rien ne met en garde contre sa toxicité. Il n'exhale point, quoiqu'on ait dit, d'odeur forte, répoussante ; ce n'est pas un résineux comme la plupart des autres conifères, et son feuillage d'un vert foncé tente les animaux domestiques qui, pendant l'hiver surtout, alors qu'ils sont soumis au regime du sec, broutent ses rameaux et s'empoisonnent.'[1]

The poisonous effects of the leaves on horses were known to Theophrastus.[2]

The article in the *Encyclopædia Britannica* says that 'if cut and laid in heaps to undergo fermentation it is very injurious,' but it cannot be supposed that the poisonous properties would be increased by fermentation, and it seems more probable that the sweetness thus caused renders it attractive to cattle, and induces them to eat it in larger quantity than they might otherwise do. Cattle only suffer from eating it in too large quantity, either after it has fermented, or when they have been kept from green food for a lengthened time.

Some people are of opinion that the partially dried leaves are more poisonous than when green, but there can be no good reason for this. Professor Munro says:[3] 'Also the half-dried leaves would be, *ceteris paribus*, more potent than the fresh'— a statement which is not very clear in its meaning, but if it implies that a given quantity is more poisonous when half-dried than when fresh, it is open to question, for it is difficult to see how the desiccation can increase the amount of poison any more than fermentation would.

---

[1] *Des Plantes Vénéneuses.*   [2] Lib. iii.
[3] *Journ. Roy. Agric. Soc.*

'Further and extended chemical researches, in conjunction with physiological experiments, are necessary to clear up the matter.'

Evelyn remarks:[1] 'I marvel there are no more such effects of it, both horses and other cattle being free to browse on it, where it naturally grows.'

On inquiring of a very intelligent resident at Tintern whether cattle suffered from eating the yew, so abundant in the vicinity, he replied that they never ate sufficient to injure them unless it was cut. And an old shepherd on Box Hill told me that his cows frequently ate the leaves of this tree, but never took any harm from it, as they were turned out daily, and therefore never took a hurtful quantity.

When they have been shut up, and especially when the ground is covered with snow, the result is very different, as they eat greedily of the only green thing visible. Thus in January 1823, in a deep snow, Messrs. Woodward and Chelmsford[2] turned out three healthy horses into a small close, adjoining which was a yew-tree. In three hours they were found dead with yew in their stomachs.

'Master Wells, minister at Adderbury, seeing some Boyes breaking Boughs from the Yew tree in the churchyard, thought himself much injured. To prevent the like Trespasses, he sent one presently to cut downe the tree and to bring it in . . .

[1] *Sylva*, 1812, p. 266. [2] Withering.

his cowes began to feed upon the Leaves, and two of them within a few hours dyed. *A just reward.*'[1]

In the *New Planter's Kalendar* it is stated that 'there are many trees in pastures and fences around, and also hedges, which are uniformly browsed by sheep and cattle without doing them any injury whatever. Marshall has seen extensive yew plantations into which cattle were admitted without any evil consequences to themselves, though the trees were browsed to the very boughs.' Many instances of horses and cattle having been poisoned by it are related in the *Gardener's Chronicle* between 1870 and 1880.

By a course of experiments, made by Professor Wiborg[2] of Copenhagen, it was shown that although the leaves when eaten alone were particularly fatal to horses, when mixed with twice or thrice their quantity of oats, they could be eaten with impunity. Loudon mentions that in the mountainous parts of Hanover and Hesse, the peasants feed their cattle in part with the branches of yew during the winter season, beginning with a small quantity, and gradually increasing the amount.

Deer, sheep, goats, hares, and rabbits eat yew without harm. Cattle and horses, if not freshly turned out, do not eat sufficient to cause any evil.

[1] Cole, *Art of Simpling*, etc., 1656.
[2] Selby, *Forest Trees*, p. 373.

Mr. Strickland[1] considers that the danger to cattle is obviated by their eating it *habitually*, and therefore plants it in pastures. In this he is probably right, but the danger remains if the cattle are at any time shut up.

Cornevin[2] shows experimentally that the quantity of autumnal and winter leaves necessary to cause death in animals is as follows :—

For EACH KILOGRAMME *of weight of the live animal.*

2 grammes	for the Horse.
1 gr. 60	„ Ass or Mule.
10 gr.	„ Sheep.
12 gr.	„ Goat.
10 gr.	„ Cow.
3 gr.	„ Pig.
8 gr.	„ Dog.
20 gr.	„ Rabbit.

From this Table we gather that the equine race is of all others the most susceptible to the poisonous effects of the yew.

Birds of all kinds are poisoned by the leaves. Pheasants are apparently the greatest sufferers from this cause. In 1892 Sir W. B. Ffolkes[3] of Hillington Hall found in his coverts fifteen pheasants which had been killed by eating yew leaves. His keeper informed him that after they have been disturbed by shooting, they take to perching in

[1] *Gard. Chron.*, Sept. 24, 1892.   [2] *Op. cit.*
[3] *Journ. Roy. Agricult. Soc.*, 1892.

the yew-trees, and are then apt to pick the leaves Other instances are reported in the *Field*, 1876, 1890-94. Mr. Tegetmeier gives a similar instance recently.[1]

Taxin.—The definite alkaloid or active principle of the yew was discovered in the leaves by Marmé in 1876.

It is a white crystalline powder which melts at 80°. More of the alkaloid is contained in the leaves than in the seed.[2] Two pounds of the leaves yield, by treatment with alcohol and tartaric acid, three grains of taxin. Strong sulphuric acid dissolves it, with the production of a purple red colour.[3]

In 1880 Amato and Capparelli obtained Taxin from the leaves and seeds by exhausting them with ether. They also obtained a non-nitrogenous crystalline compound *milossin*, and a volatile oil which distils with steam, and has the odour of fennel. 'It is odourless, but has a very bitter taste.'

Schroff considers the ethereal extract and the alcoholic the most suitable preparations for medicinal purposes, the former in the dose of a quarter of a grain, the latter in doses of one or two grains. The pure alkaloid taxin yields more exact results, though I am inclined to think that the tincture is more efficacious.

[1] *Field*, Nov. 28, 1896.   [2] Thorpe's *Dict. of Applied Chemistry*, 1042.
[3] Lucas, *Arch. Pharm.* (2) lxxxv, 145.

Poisonous effects on animals

Taxin is insoluble in water—a fact which renders useless all the experiments that have been made with watery extracts of the leaves. Cornevin[1] proved this by administering to a horse the liquid from a prolonged maceration of the leaves, which did not cause any untoward symptoms, while the boiled leaves themselves produced death.

[1] *Op. cit.* supra.

YEW-TREE AT KILLYLEIGH CASTLE, CO. DOWN.
From a photograph sent by COLONEL R. HAMILTON.

CHAPTER XI

Poetical allusions, etc., to the yew in ancient and modern times.

IN the poetical writings of ancient, mediæval, and modern authors there are many allusions to the yew and the bow, mostly having reference to their deadly character and to the gloomy, funereal aspect of the tree. Thus, Homer speaks of the Cretans as being 'dreadful with the bended bow.' He makes the Greeks appear as having wonderful accuracy of aim, surpassing even that of our famous Robin Hood. In the games which succeeded the funeral of Patroclus, Teucer and Meriones contest for the prize with bow and arrow. The mark is a dove tied to the mast of a ship. Teucer cuts with an arrow the string by which the dove is tied, and Meriones afterwards kills the bird on the wing.

> 'The dove in airy circles as she wheels
> Amid the cloud, the piercing arrow feels.'[1]

And again :—

> 'Raging with grief, great Menelaus burns,
> And, fraught with vengeance, to the victor turns
> That shook the ponderous lance, in act to throw
> And this stood adverse with the bended bow.

[1] *Iliad* xxiii. 1013 (Pope's translation).

'Atrides, watchful of the wary foe,
Pierced with his lance the hand that grasp'd the bow,
And nail'd it to the yew.'[1]

When Æneas bids Pandarus[2] strike down Diomedes, who was committing such havoc in the Trojan army, Pandarus draws from its case his polished bow, his spoil won from a mountain ibex. The Greek bows, which were of small size, were, like those of the Saracens in crusading times, made of horn, with an intervening piece of elastic wood, otherwise there would have been no spring in the bow. This wood was in some instances cornel, but more commonly, at least in Greek times, yew.

Virgil makes frequent mention of the yew. He notices its elasticity and the danger of placing beehives near to 'where the yew, their poisonous neighbour, grows.'[3] He says that, through the bees visiting it when in flower, the honey, in Corsica, became poisonous. He speaks of its preference for cool climates: 'The baleful yew to northern blasts assigns,'[4] and of its dislike to a dry soil. The 'baleful yew' is repeated later in the same poem: 'Black ivy, pitch-trees and the baleful yew.'[5] In another place he describes it as being tough:—

[1] *Iliad* xiii. 746 (*ib.*).
[2] *Ibid.*, v. 196. [3] *Georgics* iv.
[4] 'Amantes frigora Taxi.'—*Georg.* i. 158.
[5] *Georg.* i. 349. 'Taxique nocentes,' *ib.* ii. 257.

'This foul reproach Ascanius could not bear
With patience, or a vow'd revenge forbear;
At the full stretch of both his hands, he drew
And almost join'd the horns of the *tough* yew.'

And again :—

'From cornels, javelins; and the tougher yew
Receives the bending figure of a bow.'[1]

The approach of the horns to one another is again described, and he speaks of the wood as stubborn :—

'She said, and from her quiver chose with speed
The wingèd shaft predestined for the deed:
Then to the stubborn yew her strength applied,
Till the far-distant horns approach'd on either side.'[2]

' To come now to the Yugh,' says Pliny, ' because he would overpasse none : it is to see to, like the rest (pines), but that it is not so greene; more slender also and smaller, unpleasant and fearfulle to look upon, as a cursed tree, without any liquid substance at all : and of these trees it alone beareth berries.'[3]

He also asserts that vessels made of yew wood impart deadly properties to the wine made in them.[4] And this is not impossible, although it is probable, as has been suggested, that the wine was made poisonous by other ingredients being added to it. Galen pronounces the tree to be of a venomous quality, and 'against man's nature.'[5]

[1] 'Cornus, Itureos taxi torquentur in arcus.'—*Georg.* ii. 48.
[2] *Æneid*, Lib. xi.   [3] Plinie (Holland), Bk. xvi. ch. x.
[4] 'Vasa etiam viatoria en ea vinis in Galliâ facta, mortifera fuisse compertum est.'—Plin. Lib. xvi.
[5] Folkard, *Plant Lore: Legends and Lyrics*; London, 1884.

Ovid selects this tree to mark the descent to Tartarus : ' Dismal yew shades the declining way that, through labyrinths of shade and horror, leads to Tartarus; languid Styx exhaling continual clouds.'[1]

Du Hamel du Monceau, in the eighteenth century, in reference probably to this passage, says :[2]—

' Les rives du Styx et de l'Acheron en étaient ombragées. Stace, dans sa Thebaïde, envoie une Furie, portant à la main d'if enflammé, à la rencontre des âmes qui descendent au séjour des ombres pour leur en éclaire la route ténébreuse et les y introduire à sa lugubre lueur.'

That peculiar luminosity displayed occasionally by decaying wood, and which is due to the presence of the mycelium of a minute fungus, is mentioned by Lucan ; thus,

> ' Fallen yew-trees often of themselves would rise ;
> With seeming fire oft gleam'd the unburn'd trees.'[3]

This condition is rare, and I have never observed it in the yew, but many years ago I saw, in a wood near Taymouth, a willow tree which appeared in the gloom of evening as a column of pale phosphorescent light by which I and my friend, the Rev. Hugh Macmillan, who accompanied me, could see to read distinctly. It is not

[1] Grindon, *Trees of Old England*, p. 68.
[2] *Traité des Arbres*, vol. i. p. 62, 1800.
[3] *Pharsalia*, Bk. iii. (May's translation).

impossible that this phenomenon is due in some degree to an electrical state of the atmosphere. Certainly in this case a tremendous thunderstorm was just beginning.

Luminosity in fungous growth is also noticed by Pliny:[1]—

'Galliarum glandiferæ maxime arbores agaricum ferunt (*i.e.* larices). Est autem fungus candidus, antidotis efficax in summis arboribus nascens, *nocte relucens.*'

Sir Joseph Hooker says that—

'The phenomenon of phosphorescence is most conspicuous on stacks of firewood. At Darjiling, during the damp warm summer months, at elevations of 5000 to 8000 feet, it may be witnessed every night by penetrating a few yards into the forest. . . . A stack of firewood, collected near my host's (Mr. Hodgson) cottage, presented a beautiful spectacle for two months (in July and August), and on passing it at night, I had to quiet my pony, who was always alarmed at it.'[2]

It may appear strange that in Domesday Book, where forest trees are mentioned, there is so little notice taken of the yew, which even at that time must have been of sufficient value to need some degree of care. Dr. Bright assumes, apparently with good reason, that those trees are chiefly

[1] *Hist.*, Lib. xvi. par. xiii.
[2] *Himalayan Journals*, vol. ii. p. 151.

Poetical allusions—Chaucer, Spenser 159

mentioned which are useful in affording food for swine.

Chaucer[1] has the following lines on the method of shooting :—

> 'T' enlarge his breath (large breath in armes needful),
> Or else by wrestling to wex strong and heedful,
> Or his stiffe armes to stretch with *eughen* bow,
> And manly legs still passing to and fro.'

Spenser[2] thus alludes to archery :—

> 'Long he them bore above the subject plaine,
> So far as *eughen* bow a shaft may send,
> Till struggling strong did him at last constraine
> To let them downe before his flightes end.'

One of the earliest English writers on this subject was Roger Ascham, who published in 1545 his *Toxophilus*, from which quotations will be found in the chapter on bows.

Chaucer also refers to the yew among other trees :[3]—

> 'With many high lorer and pyn
> Was renged clene all that gardyn;
> With cipres and with oliveres,
> Of which that nigh no plente here is,
> There were elmes grete and stronge,
> Maples, asshe, ook, asp, planes longe,
> Fyn ew, popler and lindes faire,
> And other trees ful many a payre.'

Mr. Francis T. Palgrave, in his charming *Land-*

---
[1] *Mother Hubbard's Tale.* [2] *Faerie Queene*, B. i. c. xi. 19; i. 8, 9.
[3] *Romaunt of the Rose.*

scape in Poetry (1897), draws attention to the fact that Chaucer and Spenser have described the same forest in the two following passages, in both of which the yew is mentioned :—

'The builder oak; and eke the hardy ash;
The pillar elm, the coffer unto carrain;
The box-tree pipes; the holm to whippe's lash;
The sailing fir; the cypress death to plain;
The shooter ew; the aspe for shafte's plain;
Th' olive of peace; and eke the drunken vine;
The victor palm; the laurel to divine.'[1]

And foorthe they passe, with pleasure forward led,
Joying to heare the birdes sweet harmony,
Which, therein shrouded from the tempest dred,
Seemd in their song to scorne the cruell sky.
Much can they praise the trees so straight and hy,
The sayling Pine; the Cedar proud and tall;
The vine-propp Elme, sole king of forrests all;
The Aspine good for staves; the Cypresse funerall;

The Laurell, meed of mightie Conquerours
And Poets sage; the Firre that weepeth still;
The Willow, worne of forlorne Paramours;
The Eugh, obedient to the benders will;
The Birch for shaftes; the Sallow for the mill;
The Mirrhe sweete-bleeding in the bitter wound;
The warlike Beech; the Ash for nothing ill;
The fruitfull Olive; and the Platane round;
The carver Holme; the Maple seeldom inward sound.'[2]

Dekker[3] (1603) describes a charnel-house as

[1] *Parlement of Foules.*   [2] *Faerie Queene*, B. i. c. i.
[3] *The Wonderfull Yeare.*

being 'strewde with blasted Rosemary, withered hyacinths, fatall cipresse and ewe.'

Camden relates a legend of a priest in Yorkshire who, having murdered a maiden who refused to listen to his addresses, cut off her head and hid it in a yew-tree. The tree from thenceforth became holy, and people made pilgrimages to visit it, plucking and bearing away branches of it, believing that the small veins and filaments resembling hairs, which they found between the bark and wood of the tree, were the hairs of the maiden. Hence the name of the village, which was then called Houton (a despicable village) occasioned the building of the now famous town of Halifax, which imports '*Holy Hair.*'[1]

Michael Drayton (1563-1631),[2] in *Nymphidia*, shows how the Fairy made her charm to bewilder Puck:—

> 'Then sprinkles she the juice of rue
> That groweth underneath the yew
> With nine drops of the midnight dew,
> From lunary distilling.'

In the *Battle of Agincourt* (p. 11) he tells of the wonderful powers of the English bowman:—

> 'And boy, quoth he, I have heard thy grandsire say,
> That once he did an English archer see,
> Who shooting at a French twelve score away,
> Quite through the body stuck him to a tree.'

[1] *Sylva*, p. 381.   [2] *Nymphidia, or the Court of Fairy*, p. 465.

And in the *Ballad of Agincourt* he speaks of the bows made of Spanish yew :—

'Fair stood the wind for France,
As we our sails advance,
Nor now to prove our chance,
 Longer will tarry;

But putting to the main,
At Kaux, the mouth of Seine,
With all his martial train
 Landed King Harry.

. . . .

They now to fight are gone,
Armour on armour shone,
Drum now to drum did groan,
 To hear, was wonder;
That with the cries they make,
The very earth did shake,
Trumpet to trumpet spake,
 Thunder to thunder.

. . . .

With Spanish yew so strong,
Arrows a cloth-yard long,
That like to serpents stung,
 Piercing the weather:
None from his fellow starts,
But playing manly parts,
And like true English hearts,
 Stuck close together.'

The preceding lines indicate, I think, the probable source from which Lord Tennyson derived the metre of 'The Charge of the Light Brigade.' The second fine stanza is sufficient to prove this, even though there were not the well-known coincidence in the date of the battle, October 15 (St. Crispin's Day) :—

> 'Upon Saint Crispin's day
> Fought was this noble fray,
> And Fame did not delay,
>   To England to carry;
> O, when shall English men,
> With such acts fill a pen,
> Or England breed again
>   Such a King Harry?'

It may be, however, that Lord Tennyson had in mind the poem of Thomas Heywood (c. 1615), like himself a Lincolnshire man, written on the same subject :—

> 'Agencourt, Agencourt,
>   Know ye not Agencourt?
> Where th' English slew and hurt
>   All the French foemen ;
> With our guns and bills brown,
> O, the French were beat downe,
>   Morris pikes and bowmen.'

Shakespeare makes use of the term 'double fatal' in evident allusion to the poisonous nature of the tree and the use of the wood in the manufacture of deadly weapons :—

> 'Thy very beadsmen learn to bend their bows,
> Of double-fatal yew against thy State.'[1]

[1] *King Richard II.*, Act iii. Sc. 2.

The witches' caldron in *Macbeth* contained, amongst other ingredients,

> 'Gall of goat, and slips of yew
> Slivered in the moon's eclipse.'[1]

I have heard 'slivered,' meaning 'split off,' rendered 'silvered' on the stage—an obvious misreading.

Compare the passage in *Hamlet*[2] where Ophelia is drowned :—

> 'There on the pendent boughs her coronet weeds,
> Clambering to hang an envious sliver broke ;
> When down her weedy trophies and herself,
> Fell in the weeping brook.'

In *Romeo and Juliet*,[3] Paris says to the Page :—

> 'Give me thy torch, boy . . .
> Under yon yew-trees lay thee all along ;
> So shall no foot upon the churchyard tread,
> (Being loose, unfirm, with digging up of graves,)
> But thou shalt hear it.'

And later, in the same scene, Balthazar to Friar Laurence :—

> 'As I did sleep under this yew-tree here,
> I dreamt my master and another fought,
> And that my master slew him.'

In *Titus Andronicus*[4] Tamora is made to exclaim :—

> 'But straight they told me they would bind me here
> Unto the body of a dismal yew.'

[1] *Macbeth*, Act iv. Sc. 1.   [2] Act iv. Sc. 7.
[3] Act v. Sc. 3.   [4] Act ii. Sc. 3.

In Hecate's answer to the aerial spirit, we find mention of the dew which has condensed on the yew-tree :—

> 'With new-fallen dew
> From churchyard yew,
> I will but 'noint
> And then I'll mount,' etc.

Parnell,[1] writing a hundred years after Shakespeare, notices the same fact :—

> 'Now from yon black and funereal yew
> That bathes the charnel-house with dew,
> Methinks I hear a voice begin.'

The condensation of dew, which is also noticed by Dr. Leyden, is not peculiar to the yew, but is a feature in most evergreens.

As a funeral decoration we find in *Twelfth Night*[2] the Clown sings :—

> 'My shroud of white, stuck all with yew,
> O, prepare it.'

Herrick,[3] in his ode 'To the Yew and Cypresse to grace his Funerall,' writes :—

> 'Both you two have
> Relation to his grave ;
> And where
> The funerall-trump sounds, you are there';

---

[1] *The Hermit.* [2] Act iii. Sc. 4. [3] *Romance of Nature.*

and he speaks of it as especially suited for Easter decoration :—

> 'The Holly hitherto did sway,
>   Let Box now domineer,
> Until the dancing Easter-day,
>   Or Easter's Eve appear.
> The youthful Box which now did grace,
>   Your houses to renew,
> Grown old, surrender must his place
>   Unto the crispèd yew.'

And again :[1]—

> 'An look, what smallage, nightshades, cypresse, yew,
> Unto the shades have been, or now are due.'

Fairfax writes of it as

> 'The shooter eugh, the broad-leaved Sycamore,
> The barren plantaine and the walnut sound;
> The myrrhe, that her foul sin doth still deplore;
> Alder, the owner of all waterish ground.'

The alder is noticed by Tennyson in somewhat similar terms in *Amphion* :—

> 'Came wet-shot alder from the wave.'

In Shirley's *Wedding* (1633) is a scene in which the servants are represented ' placing Ewe, Bayes, Rosemary on a table set with tapers,' and one of the characters says :—

> 'Ha ye not art enough
> To make the ewe-tree grow here?'

[1] *Hesperides*, p. 27.

Gayton, *Art of Longevity* (1659), p. 53, has the following line :—

'The Ewe, sad box and cypress (solemn trees).'

Prior says of the yew :—

'The distinguish'd yew is ever seen
Unchanged his branch and permanent his green.'

In *The Maid's Tragedy*[1] we find the following :—

'Lay a garland on my hearse,
  Of the dismal yew ;
Maidens willow branches bear ;
  Say I died true.'

Browne (Sir Thomas) speaks of

'The warlike yewgh, by which, more than the lance,
The strong-armed English spirits conquered France.'

Harte[2] has the following lines at the beginning of the eighteenth century :—

'Dark Cypresses the skirting sides adorned,
And gloomy yew-trees which for ever mourned.'

Gisborne[3] writes of the yew, in the same melancholy strain :—

'Nor shall the reverend yew, the sire who held
His sceptre verdant through the changeful years,
Unnoticed stand, he has beheld . . .
Thousands entombed within his shadows ;
For ages past the sobs, the far-fetched groans
Of parting anguish ere the grave was closed,
And drunk the mourner's tears.'

[1] Beaumont and Fletcher, 1619.
[2] Walter Harte.   [3] *Reflections*.

Swift makes Baucis and Philemon change into yews:—

> 'Description would but tire my muse:
> In short they both were turned to yews.
> Old Goodman Dobson of the Green
> Remembers he the trees has seen.
> On Sundays after evening prayer,
> He gathers all the parish there;
> Points out the place of either yew,
> Here Baucis, there Philemon grew.
> Till once the parson of our town,
> To mend his barn cut Baucis down;
> At which 'tis hard to be believed
> How much the other tree was grieved,
> Grew scrubbed, died a-top, was stunted,
> So the next parson stubb'd and burnt it.'

Dryden terms it the 'mourner-yew':[1]—

> 'The mourner-yew and builder-oak were there.'

Shotterel and Durfey[2] have the following:—

> 'By shafts of bending yew
> In streams of crimson gore paid Nature's due.'

Blair thus addresses himself to the grave and yew:—

> 'Well do I know thee by thy trusty yew;
> Cheerless, unsocial plant, that loves to dwell
> 'Midst skulls and coffins, epitaphs and worms;
> Where light-heel'd ghosts and visionary shades,
> Beneath the wan cold moon (so fame reports),
> Embodied thick, perform their mystic rounds;
> No other merriment, dull tree, is thine.'

---

[1] *Palamon and Arcite*, 195 from end. [2] *Archery Revived.*

Gray makes a simple allusion to its shade : [1]—

> 'Beneath those rugged elms, that yew-tree's shade,
> Where heaves the turf in many a mouldering heap.'

In a *Letter to Francis Horner*, Sir James Mackintosh notices the shade given by it, and the resulting dryness of the ground underneath :—

> 'The Druid Grove, where many a reverend yew
> Hides from the thirsty beam the moontide dew.'

And speaking of yew-trees scattered over a hill-side, he says :—

> 'Lonely and huge, the giant yew,
> As champion to his country true,
> Stands forth to guard the rearward post,
> The bulwark of the scattered host.'

Dr. Leyden, after mentioning the oak and the apple, which he has formerly praised, says : [2]—

> 'Now, more I love the melancholy yew !
> Whose still-green leaves in solemn silence wave
> Above the peasants' *red un-honoured grave*,[3]
> Which oft thou *moistened with the morning dew*.
> To thee the sad, to thee the weary fly;
> They rest in peace beneath thy sacred gloom,

---

[1] *Elegy written in a Country Churchyard.*
[2] From the *Naturalist's Poetical Companion.*
[3] The 'red un-honoured grave' has reference to the reddish colour of the fallen leaves. Wordsworth notices this as well as the absence of vegetation under the yew-tree shade :—

> 'Upon whose *grassless* floor of *red-brown* hue
> By sheddings from the pining umbrage tinged
> Perennially.'

> Thou sole companion of the lowly tomb!
> No leaves but thine in pity o'er them sigh,
> Lo! now, to fancy's gaze thou seem'st to spread
> Thy shadowy boughs to shroud me with the dead.'

The editor of the *Naturalist's Poetical Companion* observes: 'I suppose Dr. Leyden is John Leyden, who contributed to Scott's Border Minstrelsy, whose poems and ballads were published with a memoir by Sir Walter Scott in 1858.'

In Hood's *Ode to Autumn* we find the following stanza :—

> 'Where is the Dryad's immortality?
> Gone into mournful cypress and dark yew,
> Or wearing the long gloomy winter through
> In the smooth hollow's green eternity.'

Bishop Mant has some pretty lines, showing a close observation of the character of the tree :—

> 'Nor less curious the mountain yew,
> Which, 'mid its leaves of solemn hue,
> Its sulphur-coloured anthers now,
> In clusters on the dark green bough;
> Here void of cup or blossom fair,
> Exhibits; and at distance there
> Its verdant chalices minute,
> The embryos of its scarlet fruit.'

Keats and Wordsworth are the only other English poets who appear to mention the fruit.

Wordsworth speaks of the yew as 'decked with unrejoicing berries.' Why they should be described as 'unrejoicing,' except for their association with

Poetical allusions—Keats, Sir Walter Scott

the imaginary 'ghostly shades,' is not evident. Gisborne has the graphic expression, 'looking as if clothed in chalcedony.'

Keats, in his *Ode to Melancholy*, says :—

'Make not your rosary of yew-berries.'

And in *Endymion* we find him speaking of the yew :—

'Again I'll poll
The fair-grown yew-tree for a chosen bow.'

Then Peone asks :—

'Hast thou . . .
Thy dreadful bow against some deer-herd bent,
Sacred to Dian?'

And after hearing Endymion's story, she gently reproves his weakness in love; and tells

'How a ring-dove
Let fall a sprig of yew-tree in his path;
And how he died.'[1]

Sir Walter Scott, in the *Lord of the Isles*, has the following :—

'The glossy holly loved the park,
The yew-tree lent its shadow dark,
And many an old oak, worn and bare,
With all its shivered boughs was there.'

And he has also some fine descriptive lines on the yews at Rokeby :[2]—

---

[1] *Endymion*, Bk. i. p. 730.
[2] *Rokeby*, Canto II. § ix. At Rokeby is a fine tree on the side of the river farthest from the house, probably one of those mentioned by Sir Walter Scott. It is about 50 feet in height, with an unbroken lead. On the

> ' But here 'twixt rock and river grew
> A dismal grove of sable yew,
> With whose sad tints were mingled seen
> The blighted fir's sepulchral green :
> Seem'd that the trees their shadows cast
> The earth that nourished them to blast,
> For never knew that swarthy grove
> The verdant hue that fairies love ;
> Nor wilding green, nor woodland flower,
> Arose within its baleful bower.
> The dark and sable earth receives
> Its only carpet from the leaves
> That from the withering branches cast,
> Bestrew'd the ground with every blast.'

In addition to these, he describes the kind of locality which the tree loves :—

> ' To where the bank opposing showed
> Its huge square cliffs through shaggy wood,
> One prominent above the rest,
> Reared to the sun its pale grey breast ;
> Around its broken summit grew
> The hazel rude and sable yew.'

Ruskin[1] points out 'what an exquisite chord of colour is given in the succession of the passage from which these lines are taken. It begins with purple and blue, then to pale grey, through which the yellow passes into black; and the black through broken dyes of lichen, into green.'

side next the house are some trees planted apparently about seventy years, and having a diameter of 1 foot in most cases. One of them is about 45 feet high, with a diameter of 15 inches.

[1] *Modern Painters*, vol. v. p. 281.

Shelley has the following striking description in *The Cenci* :—

> 'Below,
> You hear but see not an impetuous torrent
> Raging among the caverns, and a bridge
> Crosses the chasm; and high above there grow,
> With interesting trunks from crag to crag,
> Cedars and yews and pines; whose tangled hair
> Is matted in one solid roof of shade
> By the dark ivy's twine.'

Wordsworth's celebrated poem, *Yew Trees*, is (as Professor Shairp points out[1]) a striking instance of the manner in which the poet passes rapidly to the heart of a natural object after faithfully describing 'only one or two of its most essential features.' 'Who else,' asks Professor Shairp, 'could have condensed the total impression in such lines as these, so intensely imaginative, so profoundly true?'

> 'There is a yew-tree, pride of Lorton Vale,
> Which to this day stands single in the midst
> Of its own darkness, as it stood of yore,
> Not loth to furnish weapons for the band
> Of Umfraville or Percy, ere they march'd
> To Scotland's heaths: or those that crossed the sea
> And drew their sounding bows at Azincourt,
> Perhaps at earlier Crecy, or Poictiers.
> Of vast circumference and gloom profound
> This solitary tree!—a living thing

[1] *Studies in Poetry and Philosophy*, p. 62.

Produced too slowly ever to decay;[1]
Of form and aspect too magnificent
To be destroyed. But worthier still of note
Are those fraternal four of Borrodale,
Joined in one solemn and capacious grove;
Huge trunks!—and each particular trunk a growth
Of intertwisted fibres serpentine
Up-coiling and inveterately convolved,—
Nor un-informed with phantasy, and looks
That threaten the profane; a pillared shade
Upon whose grassless floor of *red-brown hue*
By sheddings from the pining umbrage tinged
Perennially—beneath whose sable roof
Of boughs, as if for festal purpose, decked
With unrejoicing berries—ghostly shapes
May meet at noontide: Fear and trembling Hope,
Silence and Foresight; Death the Skeleton
And Time the Shadow; there to celebrate,
As in a natural temple scattered o'er
With altars undisturbed of mossy stone,
United worship; or in mute repose
To lie, and listen to the mountain-flood
Murmuring from Glaramara's inmost caves.'

Ruskin[2] thinks this piece of Wordsworth's 'the most vigorous and solemn bit of forest landscape ever painted,' and draws the especial attention of the painter to that pure touch of colour 'by sheddings from the pining umbrage tinged.'[3]

[1] The statement 'produced too slowly *ever* to decay' is surely in excess of poetic licence, for though the wood itself is very durable, it may safely be asserted that scarcely any tree of this kind is found without decay after its second century. It seems that much of the resistance to decay is due to the dryness of the trunk caused by the shelter of its branches.

[2] *Modern Painters*, vol. ii.   [3] *V.* Leyden, p. 169.

Rogers, in his *Pleasures of Memory*[1] speaks of
'The churchyard yews round which his fathers sleep';
and in *Human Life*[2] the following passage occurs :—

'Then he pursues
The pathway leading through the ancient yews
Not unattended.'

In the poems of Lord Tennyson, and especially in *In Memoriam*, the yew is frequently mentioned with that minute and accurate observation in which he transcends all other poets. But he, the truest interpreter of Nature in all her aspects, has not escaped the tendency to regard the tree in its gloomy aspect, as being associated with the cemetery. This was to be expected in such a poem as *In Memoriam*; but how beautiful are some of the touches with which he depicts it! Thus in Stanza xi., beginning 'Old yew that graspest at the stones,' he goes on to say :—

'The seasons bring the flower again,
And bring the firstling to the flock,
And in the dusk of thee, the clock
Beats out the little lives of men.

O, not for thee the *glow, the bloom*,
Who changest not in any gale,
Nor branding summer suns avail
To touch thy thousand years of gloom.

And gazing on thee, sullen tree,
Sick for thy stubborn hardihood,
I seem to fail from out my blood
And grow incorporate into thee.'

[1] Lond., Moxon, 1851, p. 15. [2] *Ibid.*, p. 84.

It has been supposed by some that Tennyson in this stanza implies that the yew does not flower, and that his later alteration in the eleventh edition is a confession of his error; but it is inconceivable that so minute an observer, who in another place speaks of the fruit, can have been so ignorant as to suppose that the tree does not flower. He evidently intended that it had not conspicuous and brilliant flowers. 'O, not for thee the *glow, the bloom*'; but he never could have meant to say that it had no flowers.

In the later edition, he makes a change from 'the thousand years of gloom,' and points out that even the yew has its 'golden hour,' which had been lacking to the subject of the poem :—

> 'And answering now my random stroke
> With fruitful cloud and living smoke.'

> 'To thee too comes the golden hour
> When flower is *feeling after flower.*'

The difficulty which has beset the general reader is in great measure caused by overlooking the diœcious habit of the tree; the pollen being on one tree and the berry on the other. But it is highly improbable that Tennyson made the same oversight; and it is even clear that he did not, for in Stanza xxix. he says :—

> 'Old *sisters* of a day gone by,
> Gray nurses loving nothing new;
> Why should they miss *their yearly due*
> Before their time? They too must die.'

This suggests that they do flower, but, in the absence of the pollen-bearing tree, without result.

It is very possible that Lord Tennyson felt that the original lines *seemed* to imply an absence of flower in the yew, and hence the alteration to make his meaning more obvious.

The alteration in Canto xxxiv. runs as follows :—

> 'Old warden of these buried bones,
>   And answering now my random stroke
>   With fruitful cloud and living smoke
> Dark yew that graspest at the stones,
>
> And dippest towards the dreamless head,
>   To thee too comes the golden hour
>   When flower is feeling after flower
> But sorrow fixed upon the dead,
>
> And darkening the dark graves of men
>   What whispered from her dying lips?
>   Thy gloom is kindled at the tips [1]
> And passes into gloom again.'

We find the same smoke-like dust doing duty again in *The Holy Grail* (line 13) :—

> 'Beneath a world-old yew-tree, darkening half
> The cloisters, on a gustful April morn,
> That puff'd the swaying branches into smoke.'

It is the pollen arising in clouds from the staminal flowers of the tree which appears as smoke— 'living smoke,' Tennyson truly calls it.

[1] The young shoots in spring being a brighter green and becoming darker with age.

'A smoke-like dust arises from yew foliage in spring when struck with a stick; flower feels after flower in the spring-time of love; the bloom of the yew is a kindling of the tips as with fine emerald flame, which darkens again into the deep-black green of the plant's perpetual mourning. Sorrow exults over the tree as brightening for a very little time and then passing into gloom again.'[1]

In the Himalayas[2] the yew clothes itself with young brilliant green shoots in April and May, and these young shoots appear a week after the flowering.

The 'gloom' of the tree appears again in *The Letters* :—

'A black yew gloom'd the stagnant air';

and in *Orcana* :—

'In the yew-wood black as night.'

In *Amphion* the trees dance :—

'Came wet-shot alder from the wave,
 Came yews, a dismal coterie,
 Each pluck'd his one foot from the grave,
 Poussetting with a sloe-tree.'

It has been said, and is probably still supposed by many, that all Tennyson's references to the yew in relation to his friend's grave had their origin in the existence of a tree or trees of this kind in immediate proximity to it. But it is somewhat

---

[1] Bayne, quoted from Wace's *Alfred Tennyson*, p. 162.
[2] Brandis, *Forest Flora of India*.

Poetical allusions—Matthew Arnold

perplexing to any one visiting the Hallams' burying place at Clevedon, not to find any yew-tree there. One did exist, however, about seventy years ago. For the facts elicited concerning this tree, *vide* Clevedon, v. fol.

Matthew Arnold, in *Requiescat*, has these pathetic lines :—

> 'Strew on her roses, roses,
>   And never a spray of yew!
> In quiet she reposes;
>   And would that I did too.'

YEW AT S. HAYLING.
From a photograph by Mr. SCORER, Havant.

CHAPTER XII

Notes, historical, etc., on some of the more remarkable trees
in Great Britain and Ireland.

I WOULD like to preface the 'Notes' by calling attention to the serious extent of damage which many old trees suffer for want of proper protection. Children are allowed to climb over the branches, inflicting much injury. Sometimes one sees this obviated by a surrounding railing, but in far too many instances no protection is given. Hollow trees are now and again found filled with decayed leaves and rotten wood into which it occasionally happens that a match is thrown and the tree burned. In other instances the hollow is used for the storage of coals and for kindred purposes. Large branches are often broken away for want of timely support. The 'National Trust Society,' which has done such splendid work in preserving monuments of antiquity, would do well to cast a protecting glance over these veterans.

The following notes relate to some previous measurements or historical record of the trees.

They contain also a notice of several remarkable trees, the dimensions of which are not sufficiently great to be included in the foregoing list :—

Ankerwyke, near Staines, on the banks of the Thames, about three miles to the south of Colnbrook, has a yew of great size. Lysons[1] says that the manor belonged to the priory of Ankerwyke, which was founded for Benedictine nuns in the reign of Henry II. The conventual buildings are described, in the report of the Commissioners in the time of Henry VIII., as wholly ruinous. Soon after the dissolution, a mansion was built on the site either by Lord Windsor, to whom the estate had been granted, or by Sir Thomas Smith. Near the house is a large yew-tree, which, in 1806, at 6 feet from the ground, measured 30 feet 5 inches in girth.

> 'What scenes have passed since first this ancient yew
> In all the strength of youthful beauty grew!
> Here patriot Barons might have musing stood,
> And plann'd the Charter for their country's good;
> And here perhaps from Runnymede retired,
> The haughty John with secret vengeance fired,
> Might curse the day which saw his weakness yield
> Extorted rights from yonder tented field.'[2]

Magna Charta was signed within sight of it.[3]

[1] *Magna Brit.*, vol. i. p. 681. [2] Fitzgerald.
[3] Johannes Dei Gratia, etc., Rex, etc.
'Given by our owne hand in the meadow called Kunningsemead or Rynnemeade, between Stanes and Windsore, the xv day of June, in the Eighteenth year of our Reigne' (A.D. 1215).

Strutt[1] gives the following description of it in 1822: 'The girth ... at 3 feet from the ground is 27 feet 8 inches; at 8 feet, 32 feet 5 inches. Immediately above the latter height there are five principal branches, which shoot out from the stem in a lateral direction, the girt of which are, 5 feet 5 inches, 6 feet 10 inches, 5 feet 7 inches, 5 feet 7 inches, and 5 feet 9 inches. Above the branches the trunk measures in the girt 20 feet 8 inches. At 12 feet from the ground various branches proceed in every direction, aspiring to the height of 49 feet 6 inches, spreading their umbrage to a circumference of 207 feet.'

It 1877 it was re-measured by Mr. Troy, at Sir Robert Christison's request, fifty-five years after Strutt's data were taken. At the ground its girth was 25 feet; at 3 feet, 35 feet 5 inches; and at 7 feet it measured 35 feet.

On the 29th March 1894 I again measured it, assisted by Mr. Francis, the head gardener at Ankerwyke House. The base was a good deal broken away, and hollow up to 5 feet. The trunk above this point, which at one time was hollow, is now filled with a mass of large trunk-like roots, to a degree more remarkable than in any I have seen.' The circumference at 3 feet is 30 feet 9 inches; the two main branches, branching again at 14 feet, rise to a height of exactly 50 feet. Diameter of

---

[1] *Sylva Britannica*, p. 8.

umbrage 74 and 70 feet. The increase of diameter since 1822 is shown by the following Table:—

Girth at 3 feet from the Ground.

1822	27 feet 8 inches.
1877	30 feet 5 inches.
1894	30 feet 9 inches.

From these measurements it appears that in the first fifty-five years since Strutt's measurement, the tree had grown 33 inches in girth, or 11 inches in diameter. Christison remarks: 'If this rate (1 foot of diameter in sixty years) were adopted for that of the whole trunk . . . the tree in 1877 was only 564 years old instead of above a thousand.' 'But,' he says, 'so great a tree *cannot* be nearly so young; and the erroneous result arises from the measurements having been taken over the swelling of the trunk near the spring of its limbs.'

We have here a striking instance of the danger of making fixed rules for estimating the rate of growth. De Candolle's method is of all others the most fallacious, as I have elsewhere shown, and we find in this tree a good illustration of the variable rates of growth for which the yew is so conspicuous. The last measurement of 1894 shows an increase in girth of only 4 inches in seventeen years, bringing the total increase in seventy-seven years down to 37 inches, or rather more than a foot of diameter in that period, which is not slow growth, although it is slightly below the average rate of growth in young trees. The diminished rate of the last period is clearly due to the large growth of root-stems within the trunk.

Ashill, Somersetshire.—In Collinson's *History of Somersetshire*,[1] it is stated that two very large trees are found in the churchyard, one of which, presumably the largest, was in 1791, '15 feet round, with a vast spread of branches extending north and south 66 feet. The other divides into three large trunks just above the ground, but many of the arms are decayed.' For the following measurements, made in January 1895, I am indebted to the Rev. Charles Houghton :—

Girth at ground	. .	A 17·9 in.	B 14·7 in.
Girth at 3 feet	. .	,, 20·0 ,,	,, 15·0 ,,
Length of bole	. .	,, 5·0 ,,	,, 6·7 ,,
Length of longest bough	.	,, 28·6 ,,	,, 38·0 ,,
Height	. . . .	,, 37·0 ,,	,, 43·0 ,,

Six years ago, says Mr. Houghton, 'they were very fine trees, but a heavy snowstorm, followed almost immediately by a very severe frost, broke down the largest stem, and the trees are in consequence much disfigured.'

It appears that the larger of the two trees has increased in girth 5 feet since 1791, or 20 inches of diameter in 103 years, which is more rapid than the growth of a young tree.

[1] Vol. i. p. 13.

Ashtead, Surrey.—In the churchyard there is a fine tree enclosed in an iron fence. I was unable to measure it, but at a rough estimate it is about 18 feet in girth. There are three good-sized trunks and the remains of an original trunk partially enclosed by one of the others. These have a

SECTIONAL VIEW OF YEW AT ASHTEAD, SURREY.

diameter of about 18 inches. The mode of growth of these trunks is peculiar, giving rise to a very deceptive appearance. It seems at first sight as if there had been a central trunk, which has entirely disappeared. This is not so. The original trunk is the dead one partially enclosed; the others have grown out from the base, so that there is no actual centre, and it is evidently a compound tree.

Basildon, Berkshire.—A yew was planted in the churchyard by Charles, Lord Fane, in the year 1726, according to the Parish Register, which records the measurements taken in 1780 and 1796, the former giving a girth for the tree to the south of the church, of 6·3 inches in a period of fifty-four years, and the latter 8 feet 6 inches in seventy years. In 1834, thirty-eight years afterwards, it had only increased 3 inches, which points to some error in measurement, for it is scarcely probable that so rapidly growing a tree should have received so sudden an arrest. Professor Henslow suggests that the early measurement may have taken in too much of the root, or that at the time of the latter one the soil may have risen round them. This is very likely to have been the case, as he says, in 1834, 'roots lately injured by digging graves.' He adds, 'The rate of increase at 4 feet from the ground is slower than that near the root, upon the whole, in proportion of one fourth nearly.'[1] The rate of growth is, however, an unusually rapid one, as is shown by the following Table :—

	ft.	in.	
1780 .	6	3	According to Register.
1796 .	8	6	
1834 . . .	8	9	J. S. H.
1834, at 4 feet .	6	10½	
1889 .	9	10	Mr. Money.

Thus, if we take Christison's estimate of seventy-five years as the time required to produce 1 foot of diameter, this tree, with a diameter of 3 feet 3 inches, would appear as over 250 years old, instead of 163 years, its known age. An analysis of the rate of growth at the periods of measurement show some singular results. There are two

[1] *Nature*, Oct. 24, 1889.

of comparatively arrested growth, but nevertheless for the entire period the increase is above the average.

		Increase of Girth. In.	Increase of Diam. In.				
From 1726 to 1780	Yrs. = 54	= 75	= 25	=a growth at the rate of 1 foot diam. in 25˙9 yrs.			
,, 1796	= 16	= 27	= 9	,,	,,	,,	21˙3 ,,
,, 1834	= 38	= 3	= 1	,,	,,	,,	456 ,,
,, 1889	= 55	= 13	= 4	,,	,,	,,	165 ,,
	163	=118	= 39	,,	,,	,,	50 ,,

Borrodale Yews.—'Every visitor to Keswick,' writes Professor Knight,[1] 'goes up Borrodale. Leaving the Honister road at Seatoller, the mountain track over the Sty Pass to Wastdale ascends under the flank of the Gray Knotts and Brandreth to Seathwaite; and there—to the left of the track, and a short distance from Seathwaite Beck—are the remains of a grove of yew-trees as famous as any in the kingdom. It is there that Wordsworth wrote of them in 1803 (see *Yew-trees*): This grove of yews in Borrodale, "fraternal four,"—"a brotherhood of venerable trees," remained uninjured till 1883—a natural temple, or, as described by Mr. Stopford Brooke, an "ideal grove," in which the ghostly masters of mankind meet, sleep, and offer worship to the destiny that abides above them, while the mountain flood, as if from another world, makes music to which they dimly listen. But in the great gale of December 1883, one of

[1] *Through the Wordsworth Country*, pp. 253, 54.

them was uprooted; leading branches of the others were wrenched from the main stem, and although three still remain, the solemn majesty of the grove is gone.'

'"Produced too slowly ever to decay," they have not proved in "aspect too magnificent to be destroyed." . . . Mr. Goodwin's sketch represents the grove as it was before the tornado shattered it. In *Modern Painters* Mr. Ruskin speaks of the high action of the imagination in this poem, and says, "It is perhaps the most vigorous and solemn bit of forest landscape ever painted."'

Boughton-under-Blean, Kent.—In the Church Register, a Memorandum in the handwriting of the Rev. John Johnson, Vicar, states that 'the little yew-tree by the south door was sett 1695.'

The dimensions of this tree (19th October 1894), taken by the present Vicar, the Rev. J. A. Boodle, are as follows:—'Height about 50 feet; the girth 3 feet from the ground, 9 feet 9 inches; the branches begin about 4 feet 3 inches from the ground, and here the girth is 11 feet; the branches spread to a distance of 22 to 30 feet from the trunk in different directions. The tree presents a thoroughly healthy appearance.'

We have here a good instance of rapid growth within a known period of time. A diameter of 3 feet 3 inches in 199 years shows an increase of 1 foot of diameter in 61 years.

Another tree in the same churchyard is stated in the Register to have been planted in 1840.
It is therefore now (Oct. 19, 1894) fifty-four years old. It is '16 feet 9 inches high; the branches begin about 2 feet 2 inches from the ground, where

YEW AT BOUGHTON-UNDER-BLEAN.
From a Photograph by W. SCALCHARD, Esq.

the girth is 3 feet 10 inches; they spread to a distance of 12 feet to 12 feet 6 inches from the trunk.'

This is even a more remarkable rate of growth than the other, as it shows an increase of diameter equal to rather more than 15 inches in the fifty-four years. The tree at Westfelton is the only one that shows an equal rate of growth.

There is probably some condition of soil, here as at Westfelton, which has caused the exceptional increase in these two trees. A photograph kindly sent by Dr. Scatchard shows the larger tree as one of exceptional beauty of form.

Box Hill, Surrey.—A yew which I saw here in 1887 (Nov. 13), opposite Birchingrove Farm, by the side of the road leading to Headly, and about a mile from Box Hill, presents some singular features. It is growing in the middle of a pasture, and has a fine head of pretty equal boughs springing from a common point at 8 feet from the ground. At the ground, and for the first 2 feet, it measures in girth 8 feet 1 inch. Above 2 feet it suddenly expands, and measures, at 3 feet 6 inches, 12 feet 3 inches. At this point the entire surface of the tree is covered with young spray; some of the shoots have attained a length of 4 or 5 feet and a diameter of an inch or more, and show distinct coalescence at their base; but such is the dense shade from the overhanging foliage that they all sooner or later die away, or are eaten by cattle. The lower part of the trunk is smooth and polished, without any sign of spray being formed, and this seems to be due to the fact that the tree is used by sheep as a place to rub against.

1890, *April 9th.*—All the young shoots on the

trunk have been eaten off by cattle. The old farmer here says that his cattle eat a great deal of yew, and that he has never known any ill effects produced by their so doing. He thinks they do not eat much at one time, as they are turned out daily.

A very nice painting of yew-trees on Box Hill, but not including this tree, by W. Heath Wilson, was in the Academy in 1896.

Brabourne.—'That superannuated Eugh,' says Evelyn,[1] 'growing now in Brabourne Churchyard, not far from Scott's Hall in Kent, which being 58 feet 6 inches in circumference, will bear near 20 feet diameter as it was measured by myself imperfectly, and then more exactly for me by order of the Right Hon. Sir George Carteret, Vice-Chamberlain to His Majesty.' 'Such another monster is also to be seen in Sutton Churchyard, near Winchester.' Of the Brabourne tree nothing now remains. The Rev. J. T. Pearse, writing to a friend of mine (Feb. 1889), says, 'I cannot find any vestige of it left, nor any remembrance of this tree amongst any old people living in the parish or neighbourhood.'

It is more than probable that this, like the one at Fortingal, was a compound tree, consisting of a number of trees planted together, or else of a ring of young stems springing around the parent trunk, forming a circle, and subsequently welding together,

[1] *Sylva*, 1664, p. 84.

as I have seen in the neighbourhood of Tintern and elsewhere.

The Sutton, mentioned by Evelyn as being near Winchester, has no existing yew-tree. There is a large tree at Long Sutton, near Winchfield, but this could scarcely be the one spoken of as 'just such another' as that at Braburne. In 1889 it measured 26 feet 7 inches in girth, and the height of the trunk to the lowest branch was 3 feet.

Bredhurst.—The tree in Bredhurst Churchyard, near Chatham, is very remarkable. It is a fine pollard, in which I first noticed the features which gave rise to the present inquiry.

The girth at 4 feet from the ground is 21 feet 6 inches, and at 15 feet the girth is 15 feet. The original trunk is dead, but fairly sound, and can be seen through openings in the surrounding layers of newer growth. The diameter of the central trunk is 2 feet. The surrounding ring has a radius of 1 foot; the wood is quite distinct from the central shaft, and differs in colour. It, too, is dead. Some of the branches which still remain attached have a diameter of 10 inches. The third circle of wood, which for the most part is living, has—together with a commencing fourth ring—a radius of 18 inches.

This fourth ring is covered with young spray, some of the shoots having grown to 4 or 5 feet in length, and begun to coalesce at the bases, which are much swollen, but most of the shoots die off

YEW AT BROCKENHURST.

after a few years' growth, being smothered by the foliage above them.

Radius of head 16 feet.

A fine tree in *Brockenhurst* Churchyard, in the New Forest, Hants, in 1793 had a girth of 15 feet, and was upwards of 60 feet in height.[1] In 1892 the head was still unbroken and about the same height, and with a spread of foliage about 70 yards in circumference. At 3 feet from the ground it girthed 18 feet, which gives about 1 foot in diameter in one hundred years,—a very slow rate of growth.

Broomfield, Somersetshire.—Through the kindness of the Rev. Percy G. Bulstrode, I am enabled to give the measurements of this tree, referred to by Lord Malmesbury[2] in connection with that at Hartington. The girth at the ground level is (A.D. 1895) 24 feet 4 inches, and 16 feet at 3 feet. The bole, which is only 4 feet in height, is hollow and surrounded by young growth. This tree well illustrates the deceptive character of the ground-line measurement, and also shows that Lord Malmesbury could not have had a very extensive knowledge of trees of this kind.

Broxbourne, Herts.—In the churchyard, near the west end of the church, is a fine tree consisting of three main stems, united at the base, but two of them diverging and leaning considerably. The

[1] Warner, *Topog. Remarks*, etc.
[2] *Memoirs of an Ex-Minister*, p. 496.

total girth at 3 feet from the ground is 19 feet 3 inches. The main trunk measures 9 feet 6 inches at 3 feet. The others are much smaller. The church bears the date of 1522. A plate of it in the *Gentleman's Magazine* of June 1808 shows the yew-tree, but of much less size, and having only one stem. This must be an extreme instance of artistic licence, for it is scarcely possible that the two smaller stems can have grown in the space of eighty-eight years. It is fair to presume that this is one of the few instances in which the church and the tree are of the same age.

Buckland.—The tree in the churchyard, about a mile from Dover, is thus described by the Rev. W. T. Bree:[1] 'About the middle of last century the tree was shattered by lightning, which at the same time demolished also the steeple of the church, close to which it stands. To this catastrophe, no doubt, is to be attributed, in a great measure, much of the rude and grotesque appearance which it now presents. At a yard from the ground, the butt, which is hollow, and on one side extremely tortuous and irregular, protruding its "knotted fangs" like knees at the height of some feet from the surface, measures 24 feet in circumference. It is split from the bottom into two portions; one of which, at the height of about 6 feet, again divides naturally into two parts; so

[1] Loudon, *Mag. Nat. Hist.*, vol. vi. p. 47.

that the tree consists of a short trunk, branching into three main arms; the whole not exceeding in height, to the extreme top of the branches, more than about 25 or 30 feet.'

It was struck by lightning at the same time that the church was struck, many years ago. The only other instance of a yew having been thus injured is one of a group standing in a field just under Box Hill. It 'still stretches its gaunt withered arms against the sky, like some weather-beaten sign-post marking the way to Canterbury.'[1]

Two good plates of the tree are given in the *Gardener's Chronicle*, May 1, 1880.

In the year 1880 the tree was removed to a distance of 60 yards. The trunk had been so split that it had a direction nearly parallel to the soil. 'This huge tree was removed with a ball of soil round its roots, 16 feet 5 inches by 15 feet 8 inches and 3 feet 6 inches in depth; the total weight of the mass was estimated at fifty-six tons.'

The dimensions of this tree were as follows :— circumference of main trunk, 22 feet; of the upright portion of the trunk, 6 feet 10 inches; of the second horizontal trunk, 10 feet 10 inches; of the south limb forking off from the main trunk, 7 feet 10 inches; of the west limb forking off at 9 feet from the main trunk, 8 feet 8 inches; extent of branches from centre of main trunk southwards,

[1] *Notes on the Pilgrim's Way.*

30 feet 10 inches; and from north to south, 48 feet.

The tree was so planted that the horizontal portions were replaced in their original position and the natural symmetry restored.[1]

Strutt[2] gives the girth of this tree as 24 feet in 1822. It is said[3] to be mentioned in Domesday Book.

Cherkley Court.—In the grounds of Mr. Abraham Dixon there is a group of yew-trees covering '90 to 95 acres,' forming, I believe, part of the old estate of Ashurst, which in 1780 comprised about 542 acres, 'mostly a rabbit warren with a great number of yew-trees and pollards. The knots of the yew made fine wood for veneering. Mr. Boxall sold five hundred yews at ten guineas each.'

This is now, perhaps, the finest collection of yews in existence. The trees are in great measure closely packed in a valley in front of Mr. Dixon's house, so closely, that in the heavy fall of snow which occurred on the 26th and 27th December 1886, and was succeeded by a sharp frost, the trees were covered, it was possible to walk about amongst the trees underneath the snowy canopy. Fourteen large yews were broken down by the weight of snow and a storm of wind which succeeded it. Some of those remaining are of great size and remarkable

---

[1] *Gardener's Chronicle*, May 1, 1880.   [2] *Sylva Brit.*
[3] *Notes and Queries*, 1880, vol. i. p. 312.

form. Two of these, named 'The Queen' and 'The Cauliflower,' are especially beautiful; the former is 23 feet in girth and 32 feet high; the latter 16 feet in girth and 24 feet high. The closeness of its foliage gives an extraordinary resemblance to a gigantic cauliflower. It is, I believe, perfectly unique in character.

Besides these, there are others of large size.

(1) Shows two distinct trees which have grown together at 3 feet from the ground, measuring at this point 18 feet in girth; they separate again at 5 feet and divide into numerous branches, making a fine head of foliage about 25 feet high.

(2) Is 11 feet at the ground and 15 feet at 3 feet.

(3) Is 13 feet 8 inches at the ground and 20 feet at 4 feet.

(4) Is 13 feet 7 inches at the ground and 19 feet 11 inches at 3 feet.

Both the two last show an extraordinary amount of welding; No. (3) having twenty-two distinct buttresses, each ending in a stem above the height of 6 to 8 feet from the ground. These measurements were made in April 1890.

Church Preen.—In the churchyard is one of the finest, if not the finest, tree in existence. To the kindness of Arthur Sparrow, Esq., the patron of the living, I am indebted for the following very interesting measurements, taken in 1889:—

Height	50 feet
Diameter of umbrage	61 „ 6 inches
Girth at base	40 „ 5 „
Girth at 1 foot	30 „ 10 „
Girth at 4 feet	21 „ 9 „
Girth at 7 feet	22 „ 0 „

'The trunk is hollow, and measures 3 feet 6 inches across inside; it is this width for 10 feet (and will hold twenty-one men standing upright); notwithstanding the hollow trunk the tree is to all appearance healthy, and every year throws out new wood.'

The size of the tree was recorded in 1780, when it measured—

At base	32 feet 2 inches
At 4 feet	19 „ 0 „

In 1833 it was again measured—

At base	36 feet
At 4 feet	22 „

'Church Preen was a cell of Wantock Abbey; the present manor-house stands on the site of the priory.'

There are some very noteworthy points in these measurements which are not often so clearly brought into view. First, the difference betwixt the girth at the base, and that at 4 feet from the ground, amounting to no less than 18 feet 8 inches. We have here distinct evidence that the top was broken at an early period, and probably on several occasions in later times; that a large amount of young shoots sprang up from the base and became welded together to form the trunk; and that the original trunk has entirely disappeared, as is shown by the central hollow. We may further observe that the rate of difference betwixt these two points has been increased in the following degrees during the last hundred years. Thus :—

In 1780 the difference between base and at 4 feet was 13 ft. 2 in.
In 1833 ,, ,, ,, 14 ,, 0 ,,
In 1889 ,, ,, ,, 18 ,, 8 ,,

a total increase in that period of 5 feet 6 inches, which can only have arisen from the growth of young shoots from the base.

Then we find that the amount of increase in 109 years is 8·3 inches, or 1·9 of diameter, equal to 1 foot 3 inches in 62·6 years, the rate of growth for young trees being 1 foot in seventy to seventy-five years. These facts show that the base is an unsatisfactory place of measurement, and that old trees may increase much more rapidly than young ones.

Clevedon.—There is now no trace remaining of the tree mentioned in *In Memoriam*, as existing in Clevedon Churchyard, where the Hallams are buried :—

> 'Old yew which graspest at the stones
> That name the underlying dead.'

And again :—

> 'Old warden of these buried bones.'

I have made inquiries as to the period when this tree disappeared, but cannot learn anything definite. Rev. Charles Marson, Vicar of Clevedon, tells me that there was no yew-tree there in 1871, the year of his appointment.

Mr. W. W. Winsor, in reply to a letter of inquiry (Feb. 6, 1896) in the *Clevedon Gazette*, states that the present sexton informs him that there was a very old yew-tree in the churchyard when his father was appointed seventy years ago, but he does not give the date of its disappearance.

A sketch in my possession shows a tree at the north-east corner, apparently a yew. The sketch was made by a lady, who only filled in the outline, which was subsequently finished by an artist with considerable and, perhaps, allowable licence. But unfortunately Mr. Winsor's letter shows, on the authority of the sexton, that the tree was a willow.

Clieveden, Berkshire.—There is a fine female tree at the end of the avenue, near the Keeper's Cottage in the wood. It is probably 60 in height in the main stem, which is straight and well-grown, one of three good-sized limbs. The main trunk divides at about 7 feet; below this point it measures about 16 to 18 feet in girth. All the yew-trees at this place are remarkably free from the attacks of galls. One of them, finely painted by Lord Leighton, was exhibited at Burlington House this year.

Crowhurst, Surrey.—It is not a little remarkable

that there should exist in places of the same name two such noble trees as are found in the churchyards of the two Crowhursts, the one in Surrey, the other in Sussex. This identity in name has, on several occasions, led to confusion. Of the two, the Surrey tree is the larger. In Brailey's *History of Surrey*,[1] written so lately as 1850, it is stated that the yew-tree near the east end of the church 'measures 10 yards 9 inches in girth at the height of 5 feet from the ground. The interior is hollow, and has been fitted up with a table in the centre, and benches around. The roof, however, as it may be termed, has fallen in.' Jennings, in 1877, gives its girth as 31 feet. In April 1890, the Rev. Mr. Curteis and I found that it measured at 4 feet from the ground, 31 feet 8 inches, and at 5 feet from the ground, 32 feet 6 inches, so that it has grown 8 inches in girth in forty years. The trunk is hollow, the space in the interior measures 6 feet across, and there are seats all round. The shell is thin, but there is a considerable amount of living wood, and evidences of extensive cicatrisation of large branches, which have been cut away, close to the trunk, probably after a large destruction of the top which took place in 1845. The rector, Mr. Curteis, informs me that an old parish record in the church states that its girth, in the time of Charles the First, was 10 yards, and this has been

[1] Vol. iv. p. 132.

copied by Evelyn[1] in his *Sylva*, 1664; Humboldt,[2] Aubrey, De Candolle,[3] Manning,[4] and others. Selby's measurement is an error, and obviously refers to the Sussex tree.

Mr. Gill in a letter to the *Times* gives an account of this tree, and mentions that a cannon ball was found in its interior in 1820, and is supposed to have been there since the Civil War, and to have been gradually enclosed by the growth of the tree. This may well have been, when it is seen how the new tissues have spread over the cut ends of the dead branches. 'Crowhurst,' says Mr. Gill, 'is a very interesting little parish. There is a farmhouse, surrounded by a moat, held by tradition to have been the temporary abode of Henry VIII. when he was on his way to Anne Boleyn at Hever Castle.'

Crowhurst, near Battle, Sussex.—The large tree growing in the churchyard, on the south side, is said by Evelyn to have had a diameter of 10 feet.

Mr. M. A. Lower[5] observes that 'it is said to be 3000 years old.' I might say with Mr. Jennings, 'I will believe almost anything of a yew-tree, but not quite *that*.' Lower gives 33 feet as the circumference of the tree in 1870, and it is therefore probable that there was a large amount of young spray round the trunk at the time of measurement; otherwise the tree never could have measured

---

[1] *Sylva.*   [2] *Aspects of Nature.*   [3] *Nat. Hist. and Antiq. of Surrey.*
[4] *Field Paths and Green Lanes*, p. 38.   [5] *History of Sussex*, chap. xiv.

anything like this amount. Murray gives 27 feet at 4 feet from the ground. Jennings measured it at 5 feet from the ground, and found it 26½, and he mentions a wide opening as increasing the measurement. This opening is caused by the falling away of a large portion of the tree on the south side, and it has evidently increased since he measured it, as it is now (Sept. 11, 1894) 26 feet 9 inches at 4 feet, and 27 feet at 6 feet from the ground. The top has been a good deal broken and killed.

Selby, in his *Forest Trees*, 1842, says that this tree still carries a noble and flourishing head. There must have been sad changes since that time, as the tree shows every sign of rapid decay, and there is very little verdure left.

The Rev. C. A. Johns[1] gives an engraving, p. 342, of the Crowhurst yew, but does not designate the locality. It evidently, however, refers to the Sussex tree, though the resemblance is not very striking.

'Aubrey gives 10 yards round trunk,' ch. i., but this also refers to the Surrey tree.[2]

'The tree measured 33 feet at the bottom of the trunk, and about 4 feet from the ground, 27 feet.'[3]

There is a fine tree, much storm-broken, at the north-west corner of the churchyard, which measures 13 feet 10 inches at 3 feet from the ground.

[1] *Forest Trees*, etc., p. 342.
[2] Selby, *Forest Trees*, p. 374.   [3] Horsfield's *Sussex*.

There are also two other good-sized trees—one on the west, and the other on the east side of the churchyard.

The *Crum Castle* yew, according to a statement of Mr. Henderson,[1] grows on a small mound of earth, 4 feet above the level of the surrounding surface. 'Its branches . . . are now supported by sixteen oak posts with their bark on. Its height is 18 feet 6 inches; the trunk is 9 feet 3 inches in girth at 1 foot 5 inches from the ground; and the space covered by the branches is 70 feet 6 inches in diameter. Its branches are so interwoven and plaited together through each other, that it is almost impossible to trace any one of them from the trunk to its extremity. This, indeed, is the cause of the very remarkable appearance of the tree; but at what time, or by whose hands, this labour has been performed, is unknown. The tree is supposed to be three or four centuries old, and has rather the appearance of being on the decline . . . It is a female plant, and bears annually abundance of fruit. This singular tree is surrounded by a yew hedge, which is kept neatly clipped.' This explains the appearance of the tree, which has at some time been clipped, and afterwards allowed to grow naturally like that at Harlington. It is probably not more than two hundred years old.

Cruxton.—'This yew stood close to Cruxton

[1] Loudon, *Arboretum*, vol. iv. 2081.

Castle, and under its shade tradition says Queen Mary gave her consent to marry Darnley, to perpetuate the memory of which she had the figure of a yew-tree stamped upon her coins.'[1]

Dibdin, Hants.—In the year 1833 Sir T. Dick Lauder says there was a fine tree in the churchyard, which measured 30 feet in girth above the roots. Miss Carlyon informs me (Jan. 1895) that when her father, the Rev. E. Carlyon, was appointed in 1866 it had been long dead; the trunk had been taken up and placed in the rectory garden. 'There is a legend in the village that Lady Lisle was taken prisoner while hiding in this tree, which was always afterwards known as Lady Lisle's Yew. On moonlight nights she was said to drive four headless horses round it.' Miss Gray informs me that the tree was split down the centre and appeared almost as two trees. One half was blown down in 1836, and the other before her father relinquished the living. This tree is mentioned in Gilpin's *Forest Scenery*, A.D. 1694.

The Darley Dale Yew.—A female tree stands in the churchyard of Darley in the Dale, Derbyshire. Its circumference in 1836 was, according to Mr. John Eddowes Bowman,[2] 'at the base, 27 feet; at 2 feet 4 inches above the ground, 27 feet 7 inches; at 4 feet, 31·8 inches; and at 6 feet, 30·7 inches. At 4 feet high there are excrescences

[1] Loudon, *op. cit.*, vol. iv. 2097. [2] *Mag. Nat. Hist.*, New Series, 1836.

which swell the trunk beyond its natural size; but the mean of the three other dimensions gives a circumference of 28 feet 4 inches and a diameter of 9·5 inches. The mean diameter of the tree is therefore 1356 lines, which, according to De Candolle's method of calculating the age of trees, would also be the number of its years.' Mr. Bowman, however, calculated its age, by his own method, to be 2006 years.

At this period the tree divided into 'two nearly upright boughs, which reach a height of about 55 feet.'

There must have been some damage done to the tree by storms not very long before this account was written, for in 1853 it was stated by a person residing close to the churchyard, that thirty or forty years ago the branches extended to the churchyard wall, so that boys could get into them from the top of the wall and completely cross the churchyard on to the roof of the church on the opposite side without descending to the ground.[1]

The tree was measured again in 1879 at Sir Robert Christison's request by Mr. Smith of Darley Dale, who repeated the measurement for me in 1889, as, with Sir R. Christison, I found the figures very perplexing. The result of the various measurements is given in a tabular form, as it

[1] *Forest and Forest Trees*, Ingram and Co., 1853.

shows very strikingly how necessary it is to verify for oneself all the dimensions of trees of this kind :—

	At ground.	At 2 ft. 4 in.	At 4 ft.	At 6 ft.
Measurement in 1836 by Mr. John E. Bowman	27 ft.	27 ft. 7 in.	31 ft. 8 in.	30 ft. 7 in.
Measurement by Mr. Smith in 1879 at Sir R. Christison's request.	32 ft.	......	34 ft. 6 in.	......
Measurement by Mr. Smith in 1889 at Dr. Lowe's request	27 ft.	......	31 ft. 8 in.	......

(This is obviously the measurement of 1836.)

Measurement by Mr. Paget Bowman in 1888	27 ft.	30 ft. 9	32 ft. 3	31 ft. 2

For the last exact measurement I am indebted to the kindness of the rector, the Rev. F. Atkinson, who has given an interesting account of the tree in the Parish Magazine of St. Helen's, Darley, November 1888.

From these measurements it appears that no increase has taken place at the ground line during the last fifty-two years. At 2 feet 4 inches from the ground the girth has increased 3 feet 2 inches in fifty-two years, or 1 foot 8 lines of diameter, which is a large increase, much exceeding that of most young trees; a striking instance against the theory that young trees grow more rapidly than old ones. It is, however, true that there has been no more than a slight increase at 4 feet and 6 feet from the ground, and none at the ground line.

In 1885 I found that great care had been taken to preserve this venerable tree; its gigantic limbs were supported by strong iron chains, and the trunk surrounded by an iron palisade. In its interior two dead trunks could be made out, one within the other, thus showing, as in the Bredhurst and Dinder yews, distinct, successive rings of growth.

Mr. Bowman, with his trephine, cut out from this tree nine cylinders on one horizontal line, and counted on them 33, $33\frac{1}{2}$, 34, $35\frac{1}{2}$, 39, 53, 57, 62, and 66 rings per inch of radius, giving an average growth of an inch in forty-six years.

Dinder, near Wells.—In the churchyard is an old yew which girths at 3 feet from the ground 31 feet. There are three distinct zones of growth. The central one dead; the second of great thickness, with large buttresses towards the interior, which have probably been roots originally. Many recently formed roots are still spreading out in this form.

Dryburgh.—A yew stands close to the Abbey Church, 'and is supposed to have been planted at the time the Abbey was founded, in 1136.'[1] In 1837 it was growing vigorously. The circumference at that time was, at 1 foot from the ground,

[1] Loudon.

only 12 feet, proving that the estimate of its age is utterly fallacious. One may 'suppose' anything, but one could scarcely with reason assign an age of 760 years to a tree which probably did not exceed 300. Mr. Hutchison, in 1890, gives the following measurements of this tree: 'The head is 60 feet in diameter. The trunk is 14 feet 3 inches in circumference at 1 foot from the ground; 11·4 inches at 5 feet, with a bole of 8 feet. The increase in girth at 1 foot betwixt 1837 and 1890 was 27 inches or 9 inches, of diameter in fifty-three years.'

Another tree growing in the south transept of Dryburgh Abbey has its age verified by a tablet of stone on the north side of the Erskine burying-ground, which states that this tree 'was planted from the seed-bed by the Earl of Buchan, 1789.' In August 1887 it was 3 feet 8 inches in girth at 3 feet from the ground; at the ground line it is 4 feet. This is a somewhat slow rate of growth, yielding only 1 foot of diameter in 82·8 years.

Fortingal.—From details published in 1770, De Candolle estimated that this tree had, in 1831, reached the age of 2500 to 2600 years. Speaking of this and the Brabourne tree, he says 'it is probable they are the veterans of European vegetation.'

The tree was first described by the Hon. Daines Barrington in the *Philosophical Transactions* for the year 1769. Pennant, who also saw it in 1769, published his account of the measurements in 1771. He gives the girth as 56 feet, whereas Barrington says it was 52 feet. There is therefore a discrepancy of 4 feet betwixt these two early observations.

Dr. Patrick Neill, who visited it in 1833, observes in his notice of it, published in the *Edinburgh Philosophical Transactions* of that date, that considerable spoliations have been committed on the tree since 1769. 'What still exists of the trunk,' he says, 'now presents the appearance of a semicircular wall, exclusive of the remains of some decayed portion of it, which scarcely rise above the ground.' 'The side of the trunk now existing gives a diameter of more than 15 feet, so that it is easy to conceive that the circumference of the bole when entire should have exceeded 50 feet.'

Captain Campbell, of Glenlyon, assured Pennant that he had often when a boy climbed over the connecting part.

Of this tree, Sir R. Christison [1] rightly observes: 'It is not easy to satisfy oneself merely from the superannuated remains as they now stand that they belong to what was once one tree only.' There can, I think, be no doubt on this subject, and the outline sketch which he gives strongly supports this idea. 'Little information as to its rate of growth is to be got from sections of the

[1] *Trans. Bot. Soc. Edin.*

yew itself.' 'On many parts of the shell and the branch, the rates varied from one inch in 48 to one in 60, 68, 70, and 90 years.' 'None of these rates could be reasonably taken as denoting the growth of the trunk for much more than its last hundred years of life.' 'It is better,' he says, 'to use the general rules arrived at, according to which the tree in the first place is assumed to have attained a girth of 22 feet in a thousand years.' 'After that age no information yet got warrants a rate of more than one inch (circumference) in thirty-five years. Take then the lowest measurement (Barrington's) at 52 feet, the difference will thus add 2000 years to the age of the Fortingal yew, making it in all 3000 years.'

It is next to impossible to regard this tree as other than a compound one, formed either by the formation of rings of young growth or the coalescence of distinct stems arising from the base, as in the trees now growing at Tintern and at Norbury Park, and elsewhere, or from the union of several distinct trunks, as in the island of Lonaig, Loch Lomond. I revisited this tree in 1887, and found that the circle of wood had considerably diminished since my first visit thirty-six years before.

Fotheringay. — There never was a yew-tree within recent times at Fotheringay. The Rev. R. Croydon-Bennet tells me that, after minute inquiries, he cannot find any one who knows of there ever having been a yew-tree here. Jesse[1] makes it appear as if there had been one of immense size, but this is a curious instance of the way in which one mistake leads to another. He says: 'Those of Fotheringay had in 1770 a diameter of 2558 lines. Consequently we must reckon them at from twenty-five to twenty-six centuries.' This statement clearly arises from a clerical error of De Candolle, who makes exactly the above assertion regarding the tree at Fortingal, which he spells 'Fotheringall'—a word compounded apparently of Fortingal and Fotheringay. Jesse takes the latter as being the place in question—hence the erroneous statement.

Fountain's Abbey.—The Fountain's Abbey yews are of great age, and are supposed by Burton to have existed and to have been of no mean dimensions at the time the Abbey was founded by Thurston, Archbishop of York, in A.D. 1132, for the reception of certain monks who had separated themselves from the Benedictine Abbey of St. Mary's, York, in order to adopt the more severe discipline of St. Bernard, who had just founded the Cistercian Order at Clairvaux. The narrative of Hugh, a monk of Kirkstall, which is said to be preserved in the Library of the Royal Society, gives the history of the founding of Fountain's

[1] *Gentleman's Magazine*, June 1836.

Abbey, and this is detailed with some minuteness by John Burton :[1] 'At Christmas, the Archbishop, being at Ripon, assigned to the monks some land in the patrimony of St. Peter, about three miles west of that place, for the erecting of a Monastery. This spot of ground had never been inhabited, unless by wild beasts. This was called Skeldale, from a rivulet of that name running through it from the west to the eastward part. The prior of St. Mary's, at York, was chosen Abbot by the monks, being the first of this monastery of Fountain's, with whom they withdrew into this uncouth desert, without any house to shelter them in that winter season, or provision to subsist on, but entirely depending on Divine Providence. There stood a large elm-tree in the midst of the vale, on which they put some thatch or straw, and under that they lay, ate, and prayed; the Bishop for a time supplying them with bread and the rivulet with drink.'

'But it is supposed that they soon changed the shelter of their elm for that of seven yew-trees, growing on the declivity of the hill on the south side of the Abbey, all standing at this time (1658), except the largest, which was blown down about the middle of the last century. They are of incredible size; the trunk of one of them is 26 feet 6 inches in circumference at 3 feet from the ground; and they stand so near to each other as to form a

[1] *Monasticon Eboracense*, 1758, p. 141.

214   Yew-Trees of Great Britain and Ireland

cover almost equal to a thatched roof; under these trees we are told by tradition the monks resided till they had built the Monastery.'[1]

Evelyn[2] says: 'There are six remarkable trees of this sort now growing on the hill above Fountain's Abbey, near Ripon, three of which, in 1770, measured in circumference as below :—

	ft.	in.		ft.	in.
1.	13	0	4.	21	0
2.	18	0	5.	25	0
3.	19	0	6.	26	6.'

Strutt's Plate XXI. (A.D. 1823) gives five of these trees as standing 'on a small eminence at Studley Royal, near Ripon, overlooking the ruins of Fountain's Abbey.'

'One of these trees,' says Loudon,[3] 'is given by Strutt, from which our Fig. 1984 is taken. The tree is upwards of 50 feet high; and *if it existed*, and was a large tree previously to 1132, it must, in 1837, be upwards of 800 years old.'

Haydn[4] says that the largest of these was 34 feet 7 inches round the trunk, but no authority is given for the statement, and it is obviously an error.

De Candolle, speaking probably of the largest of these trees on the hill, says: 'Already known in 1133, it had in 1770, according to Pennant, 1214 lines diameter, or more than twelve centuries.'

Of the six remaining trees which existed in

[1] Dr. John Burton, *Monast. Ebor.*, 1758, p. 141.
[2] *Sylva*, p. 267.
[3] *Arboretum*, etc., iv. 2073.
[4] *Dict. of Dates.*

Strutt's time (A.D. 1823) five only existed in 1891, and of these two were dead and uprooted.

No. 1 is near the Abbey, at the foot of the hill. From measurements made by myself in 1891, its girth at 3 feet was 20 feet 10 inches; at 5 feet was 22 feet 6 inches: this greater girth is partly caused by the fissuring of the trunk. The tree has been broken by storms, and is much decayed on one side, and has a central dead trunk. From the fact of only one tree being mentioned, I suppose this to be the one referred to by Christison,[1] which in 1880, on the authority of the Rev. Mr. Brittleson, measured 18 feet 6 inches at 3 feet from the ground. If this is so, it has increased 1 foot 4 inches in girth in eleven years, which is highly improbable, except by means of a widening fissure.

It may be that this tree was one of six mentioned by Evelyn, as it is near enough to be included in the group, although not actually growing on the hill. Of the remaining trees, four still existing, two only are left standing. The largest of these, which we may call

No. 2, is not so fine as the preceding, but is still a large tree. It girths at 2 feet from the ground 18 feet 5 inches; at 4 feet, 25 feet 6 inches. It has two principal branches; the larger much divided, many small ones and much 'spray.' It, like the foregoing, has a central dead trunk.

[1] *Trans. Bot. Soc. Edin.*, 1893.

No. 3 is a much smaller and younger tree, but it also has a central dead trunk. Near them
No. 4 and No. 5 lie prostrate. It was impossible to measure them with any accuracy, as they lie somewhat deep in the soil and a measuring-tape could not be passed under them, but as nearly as I could determine they were both fully 30 feet in girth at 4 to 6 feet from the base. Above this they narrowed rapidly to half that circumference. They have three or four main branches measuring 20 to 24 inches in diameter at 12 feet from the base.

Judging from these dimensions there is every reason to suppose that the tree figured in Strutt's *Sylva* represents one of these two, but which, it is impossible to say. The one he figures measured 27 feet in girth in 1837, and therefore cannot be any of the other three which are now standing, as they do not come near to this in circumference. It is remarkable that in figuring the one, he should make no mention of the other equally large tree.

The name of Fountain's Abbey is derived by some from Fountaines in Burgundy, the birthplace of St. Bernard; by others from the word *skell* (whence Skelldale), which, signifying a fountain, was written in Latin by the monks, *fontibus*, and thence corrupted into the present name.[1]

The account of these trees given by Mary Roberts[2] betrays a fine flight of imagination. She

---

[1] Sopwith, *Fountain's Abbey*, p. 1.   [2] *Ruins and Trees*, etc.

depicts them as existing in the palmy days of Sheba and Memphis, but being still in their prime (!) when the monks began to build Fountain's Abbey.

In *Gresford* Churchyard, near Wrexham, Denbighshire, there is a fine yew, which was measured in 1836 by Mr. J. E. Bowman,[1] and subsequently in 1878 for Sir Robert Christison, with the following result :—

	1836. Inches.	1878. Inches.	Difference. Inches.
Girth at the ground	264	268·25	4·25
Girth at 2 feet	276	297·00	21·00
Girth at 4 feet	318	338·25	20·25
Girth at 5 feet 4 inches	348	365·00	17·00

The three last measurements give an average of 6·8 inches diameter in forty-one years.

Daniel,[2] writing in 1813, gives the girth of this tree as 270 inches, and at 5 feet from the ground as 9 yards 9 inches.

The tree is a male; its height in 1836 was 52 feet.

Five borings, made by Mr. Bowman, to the depth of 3 inches, indicated for each inch thirty-six, forty-four, forty-five, and fifty years. (According to this estimate a foot of radius from the outside would require a period varying from 216 to three hundred years to produce one foot of diameter, instead of about seventy-five years.) But the

[1] *Jour. Eng. Bot.*, 1836.   [2] *Rural Sports*, Suppl. p. 301.

measurements show that in forty-one years it increased in diameter 1·15 inches at the ground; 7 inches at 2 feet; 6·15 at 4 feet; and 5·66 at 5 feet. This is one of the examples which show how very fallacious this mode of estimating age is, when applied to old trees.

Guildsfield.—In *Notes and Queries*[1] a quotation is made from Lewis's *Topographical Dictionary of Wales*, concerning twelve fine yews at Guildsfield (Montgomeryshire). 'The churchyard is ornamented with twelve fine yew-trees, which, according to a document in the possession of J. Jones, Esq. of Crosswood, were planted in the reign of William and Mary, and are all of the same age.'

'Underneath one of them, near the south-west porch of the church dedicated to "All Saints," was a raised tomb upon which was inscribed the following curious epitaph :—

> "Under this yew tree,
> Buried would he be,
> Because his father and he
> Planted this yew tree."'

Hambledon, Godalming.—In Black's *Guide to Surrey*, published in 1884, it is stated that there are in the churchyard two very fine yews, one 30 feet in girth. Casual notices of this kind are, as a rule, by no means reliable, but if the account is to be trusted, this tree shows an extraordinary growth

[1] 1888, p. 154.

in the last ten years. From some measurements, for which I am indebted to the Rev. R. Phillips, it appears that this tree, which is on the south-east side of the church, now (January 1895) is at the ground 36 feet in circumference, and at 3 feet, 39 feet. 'There is a great cavity in the centre, and an opening of irregular oval shape about 5 feet from the ground. The external shell is hard, and shows vigorous growth, and in my recollection (twenty years) has increased in size. A curious circumstance occurred in the winter of 1886 in connection with this remarkable tree. The weight of the snow broke down several large boughs from both trees. One from the older tree was 38 feet long and very heavy, and though the gravestones were packed closely round, not a vestige of damage was done in their fall. . . .'

The second tree stands south of the south porch of the church. Height 44 feet; circumference at ground line 18 feet; at 3 feet, $17\frac{3}{4}$ feet; circumference of foliage 112 feet; height of bole 15 feet. This tree is very straight and regular. It has a beautifully fluted stem. It was much injured by the snow-storm of 1886, but every year repairs the damage.

Hardham, Sussex.—'In the churchyard stands a hollow and venerable yew; it measures 21 feet in circumference at the ground.'[1]

[1] Horsfield's *History*, 1835.

I am informed by the Rev. J. M. Sandham that this tree was destroyed by a storm about 1840.

In *Harlington* Churchyard, Middlesex, between Brentford and Hounslow, is a fine yew.[1] 'Chiefly remarkable for its large size, and for having once been clipped into the regular form shown in Fig. 1986.' 'This engraving is copied from a print of the tree as it appeared in November 1729; and the print is accompanied by a copy of verses by "Poet John Saxy," clerk of the church, from which it appears that it must at that time have been between 50 and 60 feet high. The tree ceased to be clipped about 1780 or 1790; and it is now suffered to assume its natural shape.' Lord Malmesbury says: 'At Harlington, in the churchyard, stands, I believe, the largest yew-tree in England. I never saw one so enormous, ex-

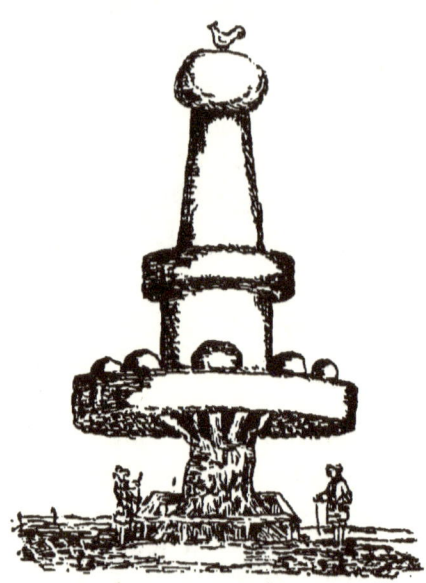

HARLINGTON YEW, 1729.
After LOUDON.

[1] Loudon, *Arboretum*, vol. viii.

cepting that perhaps at Broomfield, in Somersetshire.'[1]

In 1838 Loudon[2] says it was 58 feet high, with a trunk 9 feet, and a head of 50 feet in diameter.

Hood's lines are singularly applicable to this tree :—

> 'The very yew Formality had trained
> To such a rigid pyramidal stature,
> For want of trimming had almost regained
> The ruggedness of nature.'[3]

At *Henbury, near Bristol*, the residence of Edward Sampson, Esq., there is a yew avenue, 80 yards in length, height 16 feet. The age is supposed to be two hundred years. There cannot be much doubt that it was planted in 1688, when the house was built. All the trees have recently been opened out, and it is evident that the stems were cut down to 4 feet less than a hundred years ago, as the dead centres have a diameter of 10 to 12 inches. Young shoots have formed rings round the stem in many cases, and in several instances a second ring has formed. One of these, which at the ground has a girth of 6·6 feet, measures 9 feet at 3 feet.

The effect of cropping in diminishing the rate of increase is well seen by comparing these stems with two uncropped trees, one at the end of each

---

[1] *Memoir of an Ex-Minister*, p. 496.
[2] *Arboretum*, vol. viii.   [3] *The Haunted House*.

row. These have probably been planted at the same time as the rest of the avenue. One of them has grown into a noble tree, though it is clear that the leading stem was lost very early. Eight large limbs spring from near the ground, at which point the girth is 12 feet 6 inches. This, at an estimate of one foot in seventy-five years, would give three hundred years as the age of the tree, whereas it is clearly only two hundred.

Hurstmonceaux.—A yew-tree in Hurstmonceaux Churchyard illustrates in a more striking degree than any which I have seen, the rapid growth in girth which takes place when the trunk is covered with young spray. The two main stems have been long killed through being broken by storm. Below their point of bifurcation the trunk measures over 3 feet in diameter. Four feet below this several large branches are given off from the main trunk, which here measures about 16 feet in circumference. At 4 to 5 feet from the ground the trunk is completely surrounded by dense young growth, which has caused an enlargement of the trunk to the extent of 30 feet of girth. It is, as in all such cases, somewhat difficult to measure accurately, but with great care I managed to pass a thread round the tree close to the wood. If we allow an error of a foot, which is, I should say, ample, it appears that the trunk from which the young wood springs surpasses in girth that above 5 feet by at least

13 feet. It is probable that this amount of growth has been produced in about fifty years, judging from the appearance of the upper part of the dead trunk. The clerk tells me he sees no marked difference during the last thirty-six years, his tenure of office. It certainly cannot be much beyond the half-century since the top was broken. It is probable that these 13 feet of girth may have been produced in about the same period, for I have elsewhere found that a broken tree becomes surrounded with young growth in two or three years.

The height of the tree is about 30 feet.

At the foot of the tree is the grave of Archdeacon Hare.

Iffley.—The tree in Iffley Churchyard, near Oxford, 'is supposed to be coeval with the church, which it is believed was built previous to the Norman Conquest. The dimensions of this tree in 1836 were as follows: Girth of the trunk, at 2 feet from the ground, 20 feet, and at 4 feet from the ground, where the branches begin, 17 feet.

'The trunk is now little more than a shell, and there is an opening on the east side of the tree, which is 4 feet high and about 4 feet in width. The cavity within is 7 feet long and 4 feet wide. The height of the tree is 22 feet.'[1]

The Rev. H. Walmisley tells me that the date of the church is 1130. 'The yew is a good deal

[1] Loudon, *Arboretum*, vol. iv. 2076.

decayed, and almost hollow on one side, but there are many young shoots all around it' (A.D. 1895).

The *Inch Lonaig* yew, Loch Lomond, the property of Sir James Colquhoun, according to Sir T. Dick Lauder, measured in 1877, 13 feet in circumference. Another was 10 feet 7 inches, and 40 feet high, In 1814, three hundred of the trees in this island, which is known as Yew Tree Island, were cut down, and Sir Robert Christison had an opportunity of counting the annual rings in some of them. One of these measured 27 inches in diameter, and consequently the girth must have been about 7 feet. The section of wood measures 26 inches across, one radius being 14·14 and the other 11·86. On the former, Mr. Gordon counted 237 rings, on the shorter Sir R. Christison counted 227.[1]

The rate of growth is, on an average of both radii, one inch in eighteen years—the two extremes being sixteen and twenty. The average rate of growth for the first century of its age, is (for average, the longer radius an inch in 12·9 years, for the shorter, 14·6) an inch of radius in 13·75 years, and for its last eighty years (35·75 and 36·75) only one inch in 36¼ years.

There must have been some disturbing cause affecting the growth of this tree. That at Boughton-under-Blean had attained a girth of 9 feet 9 inches in the known age of two hundred years.

[1] *Op. cit.*

'Another tree had a trunk which was about 9 feet girth at 9 inches from the ground. Its annual rings are irregular, in consequence of there being two subsidiary sets beside the main disc, each having its own central point.' I have little doubt this is a very frequent occurrence in yew-trees, and that it is apt to lead to confusion in estimating their age.

Loudon[1] says that there has been for many years a herd of deer in the island, which has prevented young trees rising from seed. Many of those which have begun to decay have sent up shoots from their roots close to the old trunk. After a time, many of those shoots coalesce and form at last a complete new trunk, at the side of which the old one continues to decay. In this way the tree comes to be regenerated from the root.

Dr. Johnson, in his Journey to the Western Islands, writes: 'The heaviness of the rain shortened our voyage, but we landed on an island planted (?) with yew and stocked with deer.'

Kyre Park, Worcestershire.—In the grounds of E. J. Baldwyn-Childe, Esq., are two remarkably fine yews, the measurements of which have been kindly sent to me by Mrs. Baldwyn-Childe.

'In the shrubbery stands a very old tree, split in two parts; the portion on the lowest ground has fallen partly over, and so slipped away from the

[1] *Op. cit.*

upper half; the upright portion is now 30 feet in girth at the ground level, 24 feet in girth at 5 feet. The slanting portion is hollow, 36 feet at ground level, 32 feet at 5 feet. Total diameter of umbrage 65 feet.

'Both parts show great vigour of growth. I think the yew was hollow before it was split, and the interior shows fire-action.'

'Outside the "Wood-patch Grove" stands a yew-tree 30 feet at ground level, 26 feet at 5 feet, sound and growing; top not broken; with plenty of young growth. Forty or fifty years ago this tree was hollow, and an old man remembers twelve persons standing inside it, but it is now filled. It stands by the river Kyre, which divides the counties of Worcestershire and Herefordshire, and the Courts Leets were formerly held by the owners of Kyre under its shade.'

'The grant from Edward I., A.D. 1275, to John Wyard to enclose and plant the park at Caer Wyard, still exists, but neither of the yews are in the park or enclosure' (July 19, 1895).

This tree affords another striking example—such as we find in those of Ankerwyke a. d Dinder—of the rapid growth of central roots, by means of which the trunk, after being hollow, again becomes solid.

Kyre Park contains many fine and notable trees of oak, beech, etc. The largest yew might readily

YEW IN LEEDS CHURCHYARD, KENT.

become, in a comparatively short time, similar to the Fortingal tree. If it were broken away at the top, and had young shoots springing up around, it would appear as one tree with a circumference exceeding that of Fortingal.

Leeds.—In the churchyard of Leeds, Kent, is a very old tree, now in its decadence, a mere shell of the original trunk remaining. At the ground line it measures 28 feet in circumference, and it swells gradually upwards to 32 feet, at 3 feet 6, contracting again to 25 feet at 5 feet (Feb. 26, 1892). There is not very much of the top remaining; it must have diminished largely within the last sixty years, as the following measurements given by Loudon[1] show: 'Greatest circumference 31·2; at 7 feet high, 28·8; diameter of hollow in October 1833, when some gypsies had been residing in it, 8 feet 6 inches; height to the lowest branch 7 feet 11 inches; total height 32·4, and diameter of head 50 feet.'

The tree is a female, much infested with galls. In the same enclosure are three other trees, all males, none of which show any sign of galls. One of these at the east side is a fine well-grown tree, measuring 6 feet 5 inches in girth at 3 feet from the ground.

Llanthewy Bach.—The yew in the churchyard of Llanthewy Bach, near Carleon,[2] 'measures

[1] *Arboretum*, etc., p. 2092.   [2] Strutt, *Sylva Brit.*, 1822.

30 feet 4 inches in circumference at 3 feet from the ground; has a stunted, hollow trunk, with a lateral opening, and will hold five or six persons.'

'It has in the centre a still more remarkable inner trunk, covered with bark, quite detached and distinct from the old trunk below, but united to it above by a great branch running into, or more probably proceeding from it.'[1]

This inner trunk is, no doubt, like that in the Portbury and Dinder trees, the result of a root sent down from the crown through the decayed wood in the centre.

The Rev. W. A. W. Evans, writes to me in April 1895: 'Height, 45 feet; spread, 40 feet; girth at ground, 31 feet; do. at 3 feet, 32 feet; length of bole to first bough, 5 feet. The trunk is covered with young spray.'

Owing to the central roots taking on the stem function, it is obvious that in examples like this, the rate of increase cannot be justly estimated. But even here, in spite of the formation of a new central trunk, the increase in seventy-three years at 3 feet from the ground amounts to 7 inches of diameter.

Lorton Yew.—This is described in the poem *Yew Trees.* 'It is greatly reduced in size and majesty since Wordsworth wrote his poem,' says Professor Knight, 'and it is now very much of a

[1] Strutt, *Sylva Brit.*, 1822.

ruin.' Mr. Wilson Robinson of Whinfell Hall, Cockermouth, wrote of it thus to Professor Knight, in 1880:—

'The tree in outline expanded towards the root considerably, then, at about 2 feet from the ground, the trunk began to separate into huge limbs, spreading in all directions. I once measured this trunk at its least circumference, and found it 23 feet 10 inches. For the last fifty or sixty years, the branches have been gradually dying on the south-east side, and about twenty-five years ago a strong south-east gale—coming down Hope Gill—wrenched off one of the great side branches, down to the ground, carrying away nearly a third of the tree. . . . Many large dead branches have been cut off, and now we have to regret that the "pride of Lorton Vale," shorn of its ancient dignity, is but a ruin much more venerable than picturesque.'[1]

'Long after it had ceased supplying,' says the Rev. H. D. Rawnsley,[2]

> 'weapons for the bands
> Of Umfraville or Percy ere they marched
> To Scotland's heaths; or those that crossed the sea
> And drew their sounding bows at Azincourt,'[3]

'that tree listened to the preachers of peace as better than war. There, whilst Cromwell's soldiers,

---

[1] *Through the Wordsworth Country*, pp. 255, 256.
[2] *The English Lakes*, vol. i. p. 219.
[3] Wordsworth, *Yew-Trees*, p. 22.

who chanced to be quartered on that spot, kept order, did George Fox and his friend James Lancaster speak "largely" to a great multitude of people in the year 1653, and Fox, writing in his Journal an account of the sermon, tells us, "This tree was so full of people that I feared they would break it down."[1]

At *Loudon Castle, Ayrshire*, is an old tree which measured, according to Strutt,[1] in 1822, 14 feet in girth at 12 feet from the ground; its height was then 42 feet. Mr. Hutchison gives its height now as 44 feet, and its girth as 13·9 inches. 'It is said that one of the Loudon family charters was signed under it in the time of William the Lion (1165-1214).' Hutchison says it is 'over eight hundred years old.' There is nothing to warrant this supposition, and there is no reason for assigning so great an age to this tree, which might have grown in half the time.

At Loudon Castle, Ayrshire, there is a tree, measuring 13 feet 10 inches in circumference, under which, tradition says, Bruce bestowed the castle and estate on the Loudon family, and on the same spot, John, Earl of Loudon, signed the Act of Union between England and Scotland. As the former event occurred betwixt A.D. 1274-1329, the tree must have been of considerable size about six hundred years ago, which is impossible.

[1] *Op. cit.*

Lough Corrib, Cos. Galway and Mayo.—Sir William Wilde in his book on *Lough Corrib*, p. 287, says :—

'Aughnanure—Achad-na-n-mubhar, "the field of the yews"—is so called from the number of these trees, that of old grew all around this spot, and that probably extended for a long distance eastward; so that there is a tradition that the wild-cats and martens—nay, that man himself—could have walked on their tops from here to Tullokyan without putting foot to the ground. . . . Near the western entrance of this fortress (Aughnanure Castle) the last living specimen — probably 500 years old — of this ancient forest, still (1872) flourishes. . . . Passing over the Esker . . . the neighbouring townland of Kylemore, "the great wood," naturally calls attention to the spot; for around us may be still seen the withered stumps or roots of no less than twelve of the ancient yews of Gnomare and Gnobeg; and two of these about half a mile to the north of the Chapel claim special attention. Passing down the road to Lough Corrib, through this barren, grey-coloured, rocky region, without a house or living thing to claim attention, the eye falls on a lone, grey, tall spectre-like object, standing in the midst of a large field of limestone; and on approaching it, we find it to be the bare, knobby stump of an ancient yew-tree here figured by Mr. Kinahan, to whom we are indebted for having first directed our attention to this most interesting vestige of the oldest forest in Ireland. It is 10 feet high and 9 feet 9 inches in girth; and its snake-like roots spread far and wide on all sides, crawl into the smallest crevices of the crags, where,

" Moor'd in the rifted rock,
Proof to the tempest's shock,"

it broadly grew, and gaily burgeoned when the world was many centuries younger than it is now. ... It is so hard that it is almost impossible to make an impression upon it with an edged tool, and it is with great difficulty that any portion of it can be hammered off. The outer surface of the lower portion of this tree is covered with sharp prickly projections, apparently the remains of a late superficial vegetation, after the top had withered, and which contrasts forcibly with the beautiful smooth, honest bark that has so long rendered the Irish palm an object of sacred interest, and caused it to be used in the manufacture of our ancient croziers, shrines, and relics.'

Mamhilad near Pontypool.—The yew in the churchyard, as the Rev. Christopher Cook informs me, measured, in 1895, 30·9 at the ground level, and 29·10 inches at 3 feet, so that it has grown not more than 6 inches within the last fifty-nine years; but this arises, as in the preceding instance, from the fact that most of the growth has taken place

Notes—Mamhilad

within the trunk. There are twelve yew-trees in the churchyard, this, the largest, being situated near the south porch; of the others, five measure from 15 to 20 feet in girth. Loudon[1] says that at about 4 feet high 'the large tree divides into six main branches, one of which is quite decayed. The trunk is hollow; and on the north side it has an opening down to the ground, which is gradually

MAMHILAD YEW.
After LOUDON.

contracting on both sides by annual deposits of new wood. Within this opening, and in the centre of the original tree, is seen another, and apparently detached, yew, several feet in diameter, and in a state of vigorous growth; it is in fact itself a great tree, and overtops the old one. On examination, however, it is found to be united behind, and also

[1] *Op. cit.*

at some distance from the ground, by two great contorted arms, one on each side of the inner wall of its decaying parent. The girth of the main trunk was 29·4 in 1838, so that it has increased only 6 inches in fifty-seven years.

Melksham Court, Wilts, Stinchcombe Wood.—An extremely fanciful picture is drawn by Mary Roberts[1] of the life-history of an old yew-tree at Melksham Court, Wilts, which formed, as she supposes, part of the primeval forest which in ancient times covered that country of the Dobuni.

She describes the gradual disappearance of the forest, leaving the tree standing in solitary grandeur, and witnessing in turn the advent of the Romans, Saxons, Danes, and Normans. 'Still the tree grew on, and lifted up its head above the boughs of less stately trees, for the yew does not attain to its highest elevation, or rest in the grandeur of its maturity, till *five hundred years* have passed away, and when the period arrived, concerning which I shall have to speak, the tree was only in its prime.'

She then proceeds to narrate the marriage of Richard to Anne of Luxembourg, in whose train came Margaret of Silesia, niece of the king of Bohemia. Margaret's daughter married Sir William Tyndale, one of whose descendants settled at Melksham Court, and was the grandfather of

[1] *Ruins and Old Trees associated with Memorable Events*, 8vo, N.D.

William Tyndale, the Reformer. The owner of Melksham Court in the time of Charles I. found refuge in this tree three days and nights, from the pursuit of his enemies, who had burnt his house.

It is needless to say that beyond this fact, and the actual existence of a tree in the same locality, at the present time, all the details of its early history are drawn from the author's inner consciousness; as is the case with many other histories of very old trees.

The Vicar of Stinchcombe, the Rev. R. L. Blosse, informs me that the tree has decayed, and has all but disappeared, a young tree growing up from its remains.

Muckross Abbey.—'As the abbey was in existence, and celebrated as a sanctuary in 1180, the tree, which is supposed to be coeval with it, *must* be upwards of seven hundred years old.'[1] 'Arthur Young, who saw it about 1780, states it to be, without exception, the most prodigious yew he ever beheld.'

Its trunk at that time was 2 feet in diameter at 14 feet high. In 1836, 'the tree stands quite erect; the trunk is destitute of branches for some way up; the head continues to grow.'

There could not well be found a more striking instance of the error of assuming that a tree is of the same age as the building near which it grows.

[1] Loudon, iv. 2078.

It was probably, in 1780, less than two hundred years old.

Fraser,[1] about 1860, thus describes this tree: 'In the centre of the still beautiful cloister, an aged yew-tree lifts its massive trunk of 10 feet in girth, 13 feet high, throws its fantastic arms across the broken parapets, and by its sombre shade adds to the prevailing gloominess of the scene.'

The engraving, taken recently, shows the trunk to be one of the finest now existing.

Northiam, Hawkhurst, Kent.—The old tree in the churchyard is mentioned in Horsfield's *Sussex* (1835): 'A yew-tree of many centuries, standing still, by its perpetual verdure remains an emblem of the resurrection.' 'It is said that this tree, when seemingly dead, will revive from the root, and its dry leaves resume their wonted verdure.' Like all old trees, it has suffered from storms. It lost 10 or 12 feet of its top in this way twenty-five years ago. Mr. Seeley, who has kindly measured the tree for me (Jan. 1895), says that it is perfectly hollow, and split in several places, and that a fresh trunk appears to have arisen from the ground.

Norbury Park.—The 'Druids' Grove' contains a great many fine trees, measuring from 12 to 18 feet up to 22 feet in girth. They are generally much branched from the base, and have a strong

[1] Loudon, iv. 2080.

growth of young stems welded together into buttresses. There are two fine trees below the house, near the railway, of which

			ft.	in.
1. Measures at 2 feet	.	. . .	18	0
,,	,,	ground . . .	16	6

A congeries of stems (some dead) surrounds the dead trunk, which is about 15 inches in diameter, with very many closely set spurs all pointing directly upwards, a sure sign of early fracture of stem.

SECTIONAL VIEW OF YEW-TREE IN NORBURY PARK.

The following are on the hill-side :—

			ft.	in.
3. Near Keeper's Lodge, at 26 feet		.	12	0
(Top much broken).				
4. Above, near Druids' Walk, at ground			10	3
,,	,,	3 feet .	15	0
,, /	,,	4 ,, .	11	5

		ft.	in.
5. Above, near Druids' Walk, 2 feet .		10	4
6. ,, ,, ground		13	4
,, ,, 3 ft. 6 in.		16	4
7. Top broken at 10 feet, at ground .		7	0
(Many laterals) at 3 feet 6 inches .		11	0
8. ⎱ Clusters of stems, ⎱ at 3 ft. 9 in.		11	0
9. ⎰ Coalescing up to 6 feet, ⎰		14	2
10. ⎱	at 3 ft. .	18	0

11. Near Path. Two trunks united at 5 feet, lower one much broken; upper, 40 feet high, much buttressed, hollow at base, much spray.

12. At 3 feet. 22 0
    At ground 17 3
Three distinct trunks springing from same base.

13. Below the path is a tree measuring at 2 feet 18 0

Height of trunk about 25 feet, much branched and broken. Galls very numerous on both sexes, evidently very injurious, almost every shoot on many of the trees being affected. The young trees not nearly so much so, and often a tree will be nearly free, though close alongside one that is much affected. It seems from this and other instances as though the gall insects had not any great power of locomotion, and that they keep to the tree

originally attacked, increasing on it but not spreading in numbers to the trees adjoining.
14. Druids' Walk. Top more than half broken away by snow-storm, the remainder bent down to the ground. The trunk is half surrounded by vigorous young shoots.
15. On path, near to the preceding, has a fine head, measuring 75 feet by 81 feet. Circumference of umbrage 258 feet. Jennings gives 230 feet.
16. Has three trunks much damaged by galls; several years' rosettes and dead branches remaining on the tree. At 3 feet, the girth is 22 feet. The central stem measures 17 feet.
17. Measures 6 feet 2 inches at 3 feet from the ground. There are two trunks close together at 15 feet.

'There is no history concerning them which can be relied on. They are not mentioned in Domesday Book, which resulted from a census which took little account of any growths in field or forest, except those which fed swine.'[1]

Brailey[2] says: 'Many of these trees are of great age . . . and of a girth seldom equalled. In some instances the circumference of the stem is full 7 yards at 3 or 4 feet from the ground. There is

[1] Rev. J. S. Bright in a letter to Miss R.
[2] Sir T. Dick Lauder, *History of Surrey*, vol. iv. p. 453.

one yew (evidently that I have given at No. 11) upwards of 22 feet in circumference, that has had seven huge limbs, two of which have been cut off; the other five are in girth as follows:—1st, 6 feet 5 inches; 2nd, 8 feet 10 inches; 3rd, 8 feet 6 inches; 4th, 3 feet 6 inches; and 5th, 7 feet 6 inches.'

Ormiston Hall.—'One of the most beautiful trees in Scotland.[1] It throws out its vast limbs horizontally in all directions, supporting a large and luxuriant head, which now (1834) covers an area of ground 58 feet in diameter, with a most impenetrable shade. Above the roots it measures 12 feet 9 inches in girth; at 3 feet up 13 feet 6 inches; at 4 feet up it measures 14 feet 9 inches; and at 5 feet up it measures 17 feet 8 inches.'

Mr. Hutchison's[2] measurements in 1890 give, at the ground 13·10 inches, an increase of girth of 13 inches in fifty-six years; at 3 feet, 15 feet 8 inches, an increase of 2·6; and at 3 feet, 19 feet 8 inches, an increase of 4 feet 11 inches.

The latter, giving a growth of diameter of over 19 inches in fifty-six years, is far in excess of that of young trees.

Professor Balfour measured it in 1879—forty-five years after the first measurement. It then gave 13·4 at the ground; 15 feet at 3 feet; 16 feet 10 inches at 4 feet; 19 feet 8 inches, at 5

---

[1] *Op. cit.*   [2] *Op. cit.*

feet; so that in the forty-five years it had increased 8 inches in diameter, and since that time to 1890 it has not increased at all in its largest measurements, but it may be noted that these are by no means exact, as they vary in the height at which they are made. Thus Balfour gives 19 feet 8 inches at 5 feet, while Hutchison gives the same girth at 3 feet.

In the well-known publication, *The Bee*,[1] the Ormiston yew is mentioned thus :—' Its trunk is 11 feet in circumference and 25 feet in length; the diameter of the ground overspread by its branches is 53 feet; and there is about the twentieth part of an English acre covered by it. It is still growing in full vigour, without the least symptom of decay.' This was written in 1792. Its outer spread of branches, says the old chronicler, was 218 feet, and its branches fell around the trunk like a huge umbrella, forming an inner circle large enough to afford standing-room for two hundred to three hundred people. ' Here Wishart the martyr preached to an audience composed of the Laird of Ormiston, his dependants and neighbours, and in desponding strains, in harmony with the solemn and funereal aspect of the old yew-tree, addressed his last and parting words to those friends from whom he was so soon to be severed for ever. (He was seized at the Hall by Cardinal Beaton's means in 1545.)

[1] Vol. ii. p. 333.

It is believed that shortly after Wishart's judicial murder at St. Andrews, the plot to revenge his death, the leader in which conspiracy was Norman Leslie of the house of Rothes, was arranged by Leslie and his associates under the old yew-tree of Ormiston. John Knox also used to preach under this venerable yew when he resided at Ormiston in the capacity of tutor or chaplain in the family of the Cockburns of Ormiston, then a leading reforming family.'

Patterdale.—This remarkable tree, of which an engraving is given, was blown down in 1883, being then, as I am informed by the Rev. G. W. Hall, rector of Patterdale, much decayed.

The girth at 3 feet from the ground was about 16 feet. The bole was about 6 feet in length. Two old parishioners say that one of its large branches used to stretch across the road almost over the Rectory yard, a distance of 80 feet, but it was a failing tree sixty years ago.

Portbury.—There are two fine trees in the churchyard, which I measured in May 1889. The first of these, near the entrance gate, had a girth of 16 feet 7 inches at 3 feet from the ground. The trunk is hollow. At 9 feet a large root springs from the side and passes down the centre, and another smaller one starts on the opposite side at about 12 feet. Loudon says,[1] 'One of these in

[1] *Arboretum.*

THE PATTERDALE YEW.

August 1836 had a small branch from the base of a bough, which had shot downwards into the decayed top of the trunk; and which on being pulled up proved to be a perfect root upwards of 3 feet in length.' He considers this to be an explanation of the Mamhilad tree having one trunk within another, and thinks that in this way a new tree may succeed the old one. He is no doubt right in this supposition, but the condition is too rare to be of much importance as regards rejuvenescence, as there are only six instances of its occurrence within my knowledge, viz., this of Portbury, Dinder, Ankerwyke, Llanthewy Bach, Mamhilad, and Kyre.

The second Portbury tree is one of the most remarkable I have seen, as it has a straight trunk of about 20 feet high, measuring at the ground 17 feet 3 inches, at 3 feet, 15 feet 10 inches, and at 6 feet, 14 feet in girth.

I cannot quite follow Dr. Christison's measurements of these trees, which he says are 'the one 15 feet and the other 17 feet in girth at 5 feet up.' It is possible he may have, as I did in the first instance, obtained them from a third person. These measurements, which I found very incorrect, gave the girth of the first tree as 19 feet at 7 feet from the ground, and the second as being 18 feet in girth, which it is not.

In *Puckington* Churchyard, near Ilminster, Somersetshire, there is a yew-tree which exhibits a remarkable rapidity of growth. The Rev. W. H. Box, rector of this parish, informs me that an entry in the Parish Register shows that it was planted in 1724. At the present time, therefore (February 1895), it is probably about 175 years old, allowing it to be about four years old when planted.

This tree gives a diameter of 4 feet 3 inches, which is more than double the ordinary rate of growth.

The *Ribbesford* yew, near Bewdley, 'grows out of a pollard oak, the circumference of the trunk of which at the ground is 17 feet, and its height 20 feet.'[1]

Mrs. Wakeman-Newport sends me the following account of it from a local publication :—

'*A grand natural curiosity on the glebe land of Ribbesford.*—A large yew-tree grew out of the trunk of an oak; the oak was 15 feet in circumference, the yew is 7 feet in circumference and 8 feet high in the trunk, and is still standing.'

'The present trunk of the yew was formerly the roots which grew in the oak, and still retains the appearance of the roots twisted together. The oak must be probably a thousand years old or upwards, as it was apparently an old pollard oak when the yew berry was dropped into it, and the yew, which is a tree of very slow growth in the best situations,

[1] Loudon, *Arboretum*, etc., 1836.

must have required several centuries to reach its present size.'

'*About thirty years ago the yew burst one side of the oak.* It is now blown entirely away in this hurricane, with 2468 trees in Ribbesford, Bewdley, and Dowles' (July 6th, 1845).

Roseneath.—' Between the parish church of Roseneath and the Clachan House—an old dowerhouse of the Argyll family—there is an avenue of magnificent yew-trees; twenty-one are still standing; there have apparently been twenty-four. The largest is 12 feet in circumference about 4 or 5 feet from the ground below where the branches spring. The remains of a larger one are visible, which fell some years ago, and which was cut across to ascertain the age. The age thus estimated was 240 years. The largest, where "it comes out of the ground, has many sustaining bulwarks; the girth, measured by string outside these is 17 feet. About a foot from the ground it is 12 feet. The bole of all the trees is more or less fluted. . . ." Of all the endless crops of yew berries that ripen year after year and fall, none seem to spring again.'

The roots are much exposed, and thus the measurement at the ground level would far exceed that of the tree at a somewhat higher point.

Sanderstead, Croydon.—In the churchyard are three yew-trees, one of them of considerable size, measuring 40 feet in height, the girth at the ground level being 14 feet, and the same at 3 feet; the spread of foliage is 65 feet from east to west and 78 from north to south, the length of the bole 10 feet. The tree is quite hollow, with a large opening on the west side, but the shell of the tree is thick and healthy-looking, and small sprigs are shooting out all over it.

'The church,' says the Rev. H. L. Maud, who has kindly furnished the above details, 'stands upon the site of a much older edifice, and the whole parish used to belong to the abbots of Winchester.'

I measured these in 1895, and the larger tree (No. 1) then girthed:—

1. At ground line, 15 feet 4 inches; at 3 feet, 12 feet 8 inches; at 4 feet, 16 feet 4 inches. The interior is hollow below, but nearly closed in by new wood up to 12 feet. This tree is on the south side of the church.

2. Close to the preceding is another, 6 feet 9 inches at 3 feet.

3, at the east end of the church, measures at the ground 11·6 inches and 12 feet at 3 feet. There are three dead branches in the interior. Two trunks united up to 4 feet, then divide into six large branches; apparent height, 30 feet; diameter of umbrage, 61 feet.

There are some fine yews by the roadside, betwixt Sanderstead and the railway station, about

9 feet in girth. All these show signs of having suffered severely by last winter's frost, the leaves being shrivelled and brown.

Shorne.—1. A tree growing (1889) in a plantation, in the grounds of Isaac Winch, Esq., Court Lodge, Shorne, near Gravesend, is a good example of the effects which are produced by fracture of the main stem. The central trunk, which is a foot in diameter, has been broken off at seven feet from the ground, and is wholly dead.

A vigorous growth of young wood surrounds it to the height of 4 feet, where the swell of the branches begins to overlap parts of the old trunk. The branches are of good size, measuring from 6 to 8 inches in diameter. The whole trunk is 9 feet in girth. The dead stem might be about seventy-five years old when it died, and the new growth would be produced in about the same time. Thus, the 3 feet of diameter, instead of being 225 years old, would be only 150.

2. In Shorne Churchyard are two yews of good size, each in its way well illustrating the effects of pollarding. The first, on the east side of the churchyard, is 12 feet in girth at 2 feet from the ground, and has the original trunk still standing, though long since dead. At seven feet from the ground it bifurcates, the two stems reaching a height of nearly 20 feet. These show very clearly that their tops were broken comparatively early,

as the stems are thickened near their summit, and display over their whole surface a close series of short spurs, varying in diameter from 1 to 3 inches, and all pointing directly upwards, a condition only produced by pollarding, all ordinary branches being given off at a much larger angle. An incomplete outer ring of growth has formed, and one trunk of a foot in diameter is about 20 feet high.

3. The second of these trees, on the west, which has a girth of 17 feet at 3 feet from the ground has the original trunk still remaining, and although dead, it is fairly sound. The secondary growth of wood is also dead. A third ring has formed over about one-fourth of this second ring, and has grown into a stem of a foot in diameter, with a fine spreading top. At one other point of the trunk there is an attempt to throw out new branches, but such is the density of the shade that these cannot attain much size.

Yew-trees at Southmead, Westbury-on-Trim, near Bristol.—The late Mr. Badock, in whose grounds these three trees grew, wrote in 1889, 'they are all undoubtedly very old; one is gradually losing its vigour, but the other two are as fresh and vigorous as any young trees could be. The largest is one of the two latter. Its main stem divides into several branches at 4 feet from the ground, and at this height is about 15 feet in girth. It is 12 feet at the ground level.

'Southmead,' says Sir Robert Atkins,[1] 'is another manor in this parish; it did belong to the nunnery of St. Mary Magdalen in Bristol: the Prioress did grant a long lease of this manor to Thos. Haines, Esq., who obtained the reversion from King Henry VIII.,' etc.

Speldhurst Churchyard, Kent.—A tree about 25 feet high, measures 18 feet 6 at 3 feet from the ground. At 10 feet it is about 3 feet in girth. The top has been broken. This is a good example of the rapid growth of the trunk after fracture of the leading stem. The galls on it are numerous.

Stanstead, Kent.—In the churchyard is a remarkably fine tree, with a splendid head 30 feet in height; diameter of umbrage, 57 feet. The girth at the ground is 23·7; at 3 feet, 25·7; at 5 feet, 26 feet. There is a central hollow containing a dead trunk about 5 feet in diameter, and a network of roots of good size which have intertwined and coalesced in a striking manner, somewhat like that in the Ankerwyke tree. There are six principal branches, 5 to 8 feet in girth, each enclosing a dead branch of the original trunk. In this respect this is a more singular one than any I have seen. One or two of the branches have somewhat separated from the others and have thus increased the larger girth. They are held together by chains (September 28th, 1892).

[1] *History of Gloucestershire*, 1768, p. 423.

Tandridge Yew, Surrey.—A splendid tree, but inferior to its neighbour at Crowhurst in point of age. Its main trunk is hollow, the interior cavity on its longest diameter being about 5 feet. Its girth at 4 feet is 21 feet (April 8th, 1890). Two lateral trunks springing from the base, but slightly united to the central one, are of great size, that on the south being 10 feet in girth at 3 feet from the ground, the other being 13 feet 4 inches at 5 feet. These have probably grown after the main stem had been fractured at some early period; for though they suggest the possibility of three trees having grown together, this is not probable, as they would have been of such widely different ages. There is a magnificent head of foliage extending over 80 feet in diameter. The entire girth of the trunks at 2 feet from the ground is 30 feet 4 inches.

Tintern.—The trees are not remarkable for size, but present some considerable points of interest, not the least of which is their number. They abound amongst the rocks on either side of the valley, where they are protected from the depredations of cattle. The finest tree is in the churchyard. This measures 17 feet 9 inches at the ground level. About a mile from the village, on the way to the Wyndcliff, is a tree presenting a striking instance of one way in which compound trees are formed. It has a dead trunk, the diameter of which

YEW-TREE AT TISBURY.

is one foot, and therefore betwixt sixty and seventy years old. It has probably been dead about twelve or fifteen years. From the base there spring two circles of young trees, from 2 to 4 inches in diameter, and about 10 to 12 feet high. These have a combined girth of 15 feet. They are not far distant from each other, and will probably, in fifty or sixty years, have coalesced into a single trunk, measuring 18 feet in girth or 6 feet in diameter, and showing an apparent age of upwards of 430 years, instead of about 150.

Two others, near the same place, and probably about the same age, measure, the one (with an unbroken lead) 5 feet 6 inches at the ground level, the other (with the lead broken) 8 feet at the same level. The latter has five large branches springing from a foot above the ground.

On the Wyndcliff, above the moss house, is a tree which has a girth of 8 feet 10 inches at the base; 9 feet 7 inches at 6 feet. The top is broken at 10 feet. From this point three branches spring, one of them having a diameter of $1\frac{1}{2}$ feet. Another measures 15 feet 6 inches at the ground. Most of the trees in this locality are much damaged by galls (p. 70).

Tisbury Yew.—Sir T. Dick Lauder says:[1]—' In the churchyard of Tisbury, Wiltshire, there is now standing, and in fine foliage, although the trunk

[1] Gilpin's edition, 1834.

is quite hollow, an immense yew-tree, which measures 37 feet in circumference and the limbs are proportionately large. The tree is entered by means of a rustic gate; and seventeen persons lately breakfasted in its interior. *It is said to have been planted many generations ago by the Arundel family.'*

This tree would have a diameter of 148 inches, or 1756 lines, which, on De Candolle's reckoning, would give as many years of age,—a tolerable antiquity for the member of the Arundel family who planted it.

A more recent measurement, kindly made for me by the Rev. Henry Morland, gives the girth as 31 feet at the ground and $30\frac{1}{2}$ at 3 feet. There is a considerable amount of young growth round the trunk, which no doubt, as in many other instances, accounts for the discrepancy in the measurements. There may have been internal growth as well, reducing the size of the cavity, for Mr. Morland says that now 'nine persons can stand inside.'

Trentham.—In Morris's *County Seats of Great Britain* there is mention of 'the hollow trunk of an ancient yew, but still bearing several branches.' This tree is one of a large number (twenty-three) which have been planted on the four sides of a square field. The one alluded to above occupies one corner of the field. The Rev. E. Pigott, Vicar of Trentham, has been good enough to send me

(A) YEW-TREE AT TRENTHAM.

From a photograph by Miss Pigott.

some measurements and photographs of this (A) and two other large ones, in this group (B and C).

			ft.	in.		ft.	in.
A measures at the ground			16	3	at 3 feet	13	6
B	,,	,,	12	9	,,	12	3
C	,,	,,	33	4	,,	17	6

(B) YEW AT TRENTHAM.
From a Photograph by MISS PIGOTT.

The photographs of C show a magnificent tree with a fine head of foliage.

'The oldest of all,' he says, 'stands not with these but in Trentham Churchyard.'

(C) YEW AT TRENTHAM.
From a Photograph by Miss Pigott.

Tytherley. — According to Loudon,[1] there are two yew-trees in the churchyard at Queenwood, near Tytherley, in Wiltshire, *which are above five hundred years*; the largest is 28 feet high; diameter of trunk 3 feet 6 inches, and of the head 50 feet.' According to Christison's rate of growth, this diameter would make the trees 262 years old

[1] *Arboretum,* vol. iv. 2075.

instead of 500, and it is possible that they might be even less than this. He says further : ' There is, in the same wood, an avenue 414 yards long, consisting of 162 yew-trees, which are supposed to be about 200 years old. They average 30 feet high, with trunks about 2 feet in diameter at 2 feet from the ground ; and heads 30 feet in diameter.' By the same method of computation these trees would be 150 years old, and not 200. The next passage, saying, 'Another avenue, planted about 160 years ago, and 400 yards long, consists of 120 trees, averaging about 24 feet high, with trunks about 2 feet in diameter,' is pretty good proof of the accuracy of this estimate.

Ulcombe, near Maidstone.—In the churchyard are four yew-trees, three of which are of unusual size. The following are their measurements, which I took (Sept. 27th, 1892) :—

No. 1, near the west end of the church, is 35 feet in girth at 3 feet from the ground. The central stem, which is much gnarled, and covered with short dead branches, measured at 17 feet, 10 feet 3 inches in circumference. The height is about 27 feet. Three years ago a large branch about 3 feet in diameter was blown off. Much spray and many bosses are found on the trunk, and the shoots are much infested with galls both in this tree and in

No. 2, at the east end, which is a female,

measuring 26 feet 3 inches at 3 feet from the ground. It has four principal branches, the largest of which measures 5 feet 3 inches in girth at 16 feet.

No. 3 measures 20 feet 5 inches at 4 feet from the ground. There are many branches and much spray; the top is much broken.

No. 4, Girth about 12 feet.

'At *Watcombe*, a lone farm on the road from Hungerford to Wantage, there is,' says a writer to the *Times* (1890), 'a very interesting group of venerable yews, on the site of a cell or grange, with a church attached, belonging in pre-Reformation days to the Benedictine Monastery of Hurley, to which house it may have been given by Geoffrey de Mandeville about 1086, and mentioned in Pipe Rolls as being the charge of a provost in 1156.'

These yews are planted in double rows forming alleys. The enclosure from 'time out of mind' has been known by the country people as 'Paradise.' A pair of yews a little to the rear of Paradise are known as Adam and Eve. They are male and female, 'Adam' being of a darker shade than his companion 'Eve.' The former measures over 9 feet in girth, and the latter 10 feet. Standing alone, at some distance in the background, farthest removed from Paradise, is the 'Serpent' or 'Devil.' This tree, the hollow trunk of which is reduced to a shell, but carries a flourishing head measuring

YEW IN WARBLINGTON CHURCHYARD.

over 20 feet in circumference, must be a far older tree than 'Adam' or 'Eve,' which cannot have been planted much over two hundred years.

Westfelton, near Shrewsbury. — 'A yew of seventy years old,' says Bowman, 'measured 5 feet 1 inch in girth at 5 feet from the ground.' Mr. Dovaston[1] states that it was planted 'about sixty years ago' by his father, on the edge of a deep well which he had dug. 'The yew grew into a tree of extraordinary and striking beauty; spreading horizontally all round to the diameter of 56 feet (in 1836), with a single aspiring leader to a great height.' Mr. Bowman's estimate and measurement yield 21. inches of diameter in seventy years, or 1 foot in forty years. Mr. Dovaston's measurement was 5 feet 1 inch in sixty years, which gives exactly the same ratio of increase. In 1879 Sir R. Christison ascertained that it had grown to 94 inches in girth at the same level, or 31·4 inches of diameter, 'or at the rate of an inch radius in eight years, and during its whole life of 112 years its average rate has been an inch in $7\frac{1}{2}$ years.' 'Though a male tree, it has one entire branch self-productive and exuberantly profuse in female berries, full, red, rich, and luscious.'

Whittinghame.—This tree, which is 11 feet in girth at 2 feet above the ground, and 10 feet at 5 feet, has a bole of 10 feet in length, from which

[1] Loudon's *Arboretum*, vol. iv. 2082.

spring the branches forming its splendid head, reaching about 100 feet in diameter. 'Tradition reports that under its dense shade the Scottish nobles, Bothwell, Morton, Ruthven, and others, met to plot the murder of Darnley.' Christison's assumed rate of growth of 1 foot of diameter in seventy-five years would make this tree 240 years old, and it might even be less than this. The time which has elapsed since Darnley's death is 328 years, so that the tree could not have been planted until eighty-eight years after that event.

Wilton, Wilts.—Opposite a part of the park of Wilton House is a fine well-grown tree, probably of less than two hundred years' growth, but presenting some interesting features.

For the following measurements I am indebted to the rector, the Rev. Dacres Olivier:—

The girth at the ground level	7 feet 8 inches
The girth at 3 feet	7 ,, 9 ,,
Length of bole to first branch	29 inches
Height	30 feet
Diameter of umbrage	82 ,,

'The trunk is surrounded by young spray, which in many places has taken root. They are still extending themselves.'

This tree bids fair to attain a great girth in the course of a comparatively short period.

Windsor Forest.—There are many yew-trees near the Belvedere, though none of any great size.

Most of them are fifty or sixty years old. All these have lost their leading shoots at an early age. In many instances the splitting and twisting of the upper branches show that much damage has been done by heavy falls of snow. The 'buttressing' is in some cases very distinct, and can be clearly traced to the loss of the leading shoot. But an additional feature shown in these trees makes them worthy of being recorded. Some of them are infested with galls, to an extent which I have seldom seen equalled; several are affected to such a degree as to be all but dead, whole branches being destroyed.

These present a remarkable appearance; every twig has a rosette at its extremity. Even on living trees the dead twigs and their rosettes of three or four years may still be seen on the tree. I do not know for certain if it is generally the case that female trees are more liable to the attacks of *Cecidomya*, but it is the case here; nor do I know whether the clouds of pollen on the male plants deter the insect from depositing its ova on them, but it seems not unlikely that this is so.

Yattenden.—In the churchyard near Newbury, Berks (November 14th, 1888), is a yew-tree about 30 feet high, measuring $9\frac{1}{2}$ feet in girth at 3 feet from the ground. The ground is free from shoots to 7 or 8 feet. The branches are large and well-grown; none were broken away until the spring of last year, when two large ones were split off by the heavy fall of snow which occurred. It will be interesting to note the condition of this tree after the lapse of a few years. The branches all arise from a common point, and are of nearly equal size.

At present there is no sign of decay, and there are no young shoots from the trunk. The flutings of the trunk are very prominent, and can be traced directly to their branches. There is much expansion of the stem just above the ground, where the circumference is fully 11 feet.

BIBLIOGRAPHY

Ablett, W. H.	. *English Trees*, 1880.
Amherst, the Hon. Miss	*A History of Gardening in England.*
Ascham, Roger	. *Toxophilus*, 1545.
Atkins, Sir Robert .	. *History of Gloucestershire*, 1768.
Aubrey, John	. *Natural History of Surrey*, 1718-19.
Balfour, E.	. *Timber Trees, etc., of India*; Madras, 1870.
Barrington, Hon. Daines	⎰ *Philosophical Transactions*, 1769. ⎱ *Observations on the more Ancient Statutes.*
Blomfield and Thomas	. *The Formal Garden in England*, 1892.
Boate, Dr. Gerard	. *Ireland's Natural History*, 1860.
Bowman, J. E.	⎰ Loudon's *Magazine of Natural History*, 1836, vol. i. ⎱ *Journal of English Botany*, July 1835.
Brand, John .	. *On Popular Antiquities*, etc., 1842.
Brandis, Dietrich .	. *Forest Flora of India*, 1874.
Brayley, E. W.	. *History of Surrey*, 1850.
Bree, Rev. H.	. Loudon's *Magazine of Natural History*, 1829, vol. vi.
Browne, Sir Thomas	. *Hydriotaphia, or Urne Burials*, 1658.
Burton, Dr. J.	. *Monasticon Ebor.*, 1758.
Cartwright, Julia .	. *The Pilgrim's Way from Winchester to Canterbury*, 1893.
Chambers, Robert .	. *Book of Days*, 1864.

Christison, Dr. D. . . . 'Size, Age, etc., attained by Trees,' 1879, *Transactions of the Botanical Society of Edinburgh*, vol. xix. p. 111.
Christison, Sir Robert . *Transactions of the Botanical Society of Edinburgh*, 1879.
Coles . . . *Introduction to the Knowledge of Plants*, etc.
Collinson, Rev. J. . . *History and Antiquities of Somerset*, 1656.
Cornevin, Charles . . *Des Plantes Vénéneuses*; Paris, 1893.

Daniel . . . . *Rural Sports*, Supplement, 1813.
De Candolle, A. . . *Physiologie Végétale*, 1831.
Demmin, Auguste . . *Weapons of War*. Translated by C. C. Black.
Du Hamel du Monceau, . *Traité des Arbres*, 1800.

Encyclopædia Britannica, article 'Yew,' 9th edition.
Evelyn, John . . *Sylva: Discourse on Trees*, 1664.

Farrar, J. A. . . . 'Age of Trees,' *Longman's Magazine*, 1883, vol. xi.
Fauchet, Claude . . *Œuvres*, 4to, 1610.
Froissart . . . *Chronicles*.

Gamble . . . . *Manual of Indian Timbers*; Calcutta, 1881.
Gardener's Chronicle, 1870-90.
Gilpin, Rev. W. . . *Remarks on Forest Scenery*, 8vo, 1791.
Giraldus Cambrensis . *Topogr. Hibern.* J. E. Dimock, London, 1867.
Goodwyn, H., and Professor Knight . } *Through the Wordsworth Country*, 1887.
Grindon, Leo H. . . *Trees of Old England*, 1868.
Grose, Captain F. . . *Military Antiquities*, etc., 4to, 1801.

Hannett	*The Forest of Arden*, 1863.
Hansard, G. A.	*The Book of Archery*, 1841.
Hargrove, A. E.	*Anecdotes of Archery*, 1845.
Hayes, Samuel	*Treatise on Planting*, 1794.
Heer, Dr. Oswald	*Der Urwelt der Schweitz*; Zürich, 1883.
Helmsley, W. B.	*Handbook of Hardy Trees*, etc., 1873.
Horsfield, T. W.	{ *History of Surrey*. { *History of Sussex*, 1835.
Hutchison, Robert	'Old and Remarkable Yew-Trees in Scotland,' *Transactions of the Royal Arboricultural Society*, xii. Part 3.
Johns, Rev. C. A.	*Forest Trees of Great Britain*, 1860.
Knight, Professor	*Through the Wordsworth Country*, 1887.
Lacombe, M. P.	*Arms and Armour*, etc. Trans. C. Boutell, 1874.
Laslett, Thomas	*Timber and Timber Trees*, 1875.
Lauder, Sir T. Dick	{ *New Forest Scenery*. Gilpin, 1834. { *Miscellany of Natural History*.
Lightfoot, Bishop	*Historical Essays*.
Loudon	{ *Arboretum Britannicum*, 1838. { *Encyclopædia of Trees*.
Lower, M. A.	{ *Contributions to Literature*. { *History of Sussex*, 1854.
Lysons, Dr. S.	*Magna Britannica*, 4to, 1806-22.
Manwood,	*Treatise and Discourse on the Lawes of the Forest*, 1598.
Meyrick, Sir S. R.	{ *History and Antiquities of the County of Cardigan*, 4to, 1808. { *Critical Inquiry into Ancient Armour in Europe*, fol., 1824.

Nyman, Carl Fr.	*Sylloge Floræ Europeæ.*
Parkinson, John	*Paradisi in Sole, Paradisus Terrestris,* 1629.
Pennant, Thomas	*Tours in Scotland,* 1776.
Prior, Dr. R. C. A.	*Popular Names of British Plants,* 3rd edition.
Ramsay, Professor A. C.	*Lectures on Physical Geology,* etc., 1863.
Rawnsley, Rev. H. D.	*Literary Associations of the English Lakes,* 1894.
Roberts, Mary	*Ruins and Old Trees associated with Memorable Events,* N.D.
Roberts, Thomas	*The English Bowman,* 1801.
Robinson, William	*The Wild Garden,* 1894.
Selby	*British and Foreign Trees,* 1842.
Sopwith	*Fountain's Abbey.*
Stow, John	*Survey of London,* 1598. Thom's edition, 1842.
Strutt, J.	*Sports and Pastimes of the People of England,* 1810.
Strutt, J. G.	*Sylva Britannica,* 1822.
Taylor, J.	*Arbores Mirabiles,* 1812.
Thoresby, Ralph	*Diary,* 1677-1724.
Thorpe	*Dictionary of Applied Chemistry.*
Wood, William	*The Bowman's Glory; or, Archery Revived,* London; 1762.

INDEX

ABBOTTS-LEIGH, 82.
Abercairny, 92.
Aberglasney, 14.
Ablett, 100.
Addington, 88.
Adler, Dr., 72.
Albury, 87.
Aldby Park, 12, 90.
Aldworth, 81.
Allerton, 87.
Allestree, 82.
Amherst, Hon. Miss, 9.
Ankerwyke, 62, 80, 85, 95, 181.
Anne, Charter of, 128.
Archery of St. George, 127.
Arngomery, 92.
Arnold, Matthew, 179.
Ascham, Roger, 114, 131.
Ashford, 94.
Ashill, 86, 184.
Ashridge, 12.
Ashtead, 88, 185.
Avenues, 17.

BACON, LORD, 5, 66.
Backleton, 90.
Bala, 85.
Balding, 144.
Ballikinrain, 92.
Ballynure Ho., 20, 94.
Bantaskine, 92.
Barmeath, 94.
Barncleuth, 12.
Barrington, Hon. D., 123.
Basildon, 185.
Bedfont, 11.
Beddoe, Dr., 54.

Bedhampton, 84.
Betham-Edwards, Miss, 108.
Bettwys-Newydd, 80, 81, 95.
Bidborough, 85.
Bilton, 10.
Birchingrove Farm, 87.
Bishopsbourne, 9.
Blair, 168.
Blairgowrie, 64.
Blanchetayne, 116.
Boate, 33.
Bonhill, 91.
Borrodale, 68, 187.
Boucher, 107.
Boughton-under-Blean, 51, 84, 189.
Bowman, 43, 57, 101.
Bows, 111.
Box Hill, 87, 91, 190.
Brabourne, 85, 191, 209.
Bradley, 7.
Brady, 99.
Braemore, 83, 95.
Bredhurst, 78, 84.
Brenchley, 14.
Brockenhurst, 49, 83, 193.
Brockley Hall, 87.
Brook House, 88.
Broomfield, 86, 193.
Browne, Sir T., 97, 167.
Broxbourne, 84, 193.
Buckland, 84, 86, 194.
Buckland St. Mary, 86.
Bucklebury, 81.
Buxted, 88, 95.

CAERHUN, 82.
Cæsar, 136.

Callander Park, 92.
Camden, 129, 161.
Camperdown, 51.
Candover, 14, 83.
Capel, 84.
Carrigallen, 94.
Carton, 94.
Castle Ward, 93.
Caxton, 100.
Cecidomya taxi, 70, 259.
Central roots, 80.
Cartwright, Julia, 32.
Charles I., Act of, 128.
Charles VII., 105, 123.
Charing, 85.
Chaucer, 129, 159, 160.
Cherkley Court, 25, 88, 196.
Chester, 130.
Chirk, 82.
Christison, Dr., 53.
Christison, Sir Robert, 53, 62, 64, 107.
Church Preen, 49, 86, 95, 197.
Cleish Castle, 14, 92.
Clevedon, 199.
Cleve Prior, 7.
Clieveden, 15, 81, 200.
Cloncaird Castle, 91.
Clonfert, 16.
Clontarf, 60, 93.
Clos, 140.
Cold Waltham, 88, 95.
Collinson, 7.
Comber, 77.
Compound trees, 76.
Coote, C., 98.
Corhampton, 83.
Cornevin, 140, 143, 147, 151.
Coryton Park, 12.
Cowdray, 89.
Craigends, 92.
Craignethan Castle, 92.
Creech, St. Michael, 87.
Crom Castle, 93.
Crowhurst, Surrey, 38, 88, 200.
Crowhurst, Sussex, 89, 202.
Cruxton, 204.

Cudham, 85.
Cypress, Chartreux, 65.

DANIEL, 112.
Dargavel, 92.
Darley Dale, 48, 62, 82, 95, 205.
Darwin, 30.
Deas, Dr., 144.
De Candolle, 35, 36, 38, 40, 45.
Dekker, 160.
Demmin, 112, 113, 132.
Detling, 84.
Dibdin, 83, 95, 205.
Dinder, 78, 80, 86, 208.
Dioscorides, 136.
Donington, 94.
Dovedale, 28.
Drayton, 131, 161.
Drumsillet House, 20.
Dryburgh, 48, 91, 208.
Dryden, 168.
Druidical customs, 97.
Du Hamel du Monceau, 2, 157.
Dunganstown, 17.
Dunkeld, 67.

EAST ANGLIAN SUPERSTITION, 106.
Edward I., Statute of, 102.
Edward II., Act of, 119.
Edward III., Act of, 120.
Edward IV., Act of, 115, 121.
Edwards, Miss Betham-, 108.
Elizabeth, Act of Bowyers, 103, 125, 130.
Ellon Castle, 62, 91.
English trees of 10 feet in girth, 81.
English trees of 30 feet in girth, 95.
Epithets, 24.
Erbistock, 10.
Etchingham, 89.
Evelyn, 5, 99, 107, 126, 142, 149.

FAIRFAX, 166.
Ferniehurst Castle, 63, 92.
Fernow, 68.
Ffolkes, Sir W., 151.

Index 267

Florence Court, 20.
Forby, 106.
Forgan, 92.
Fornace, 93.
Fotheringay, 211.
Fortingal, 92, 209.
Fountain's Abbey, 38, 90, 212.
Fracture of trunk, 74.
Froissart, 115, 117.
Frost, effects of, 70.

GALEN, 156.
Galls, 70.
Gamble, 27.
Gartnamara, 93.
Gayton, 167.
Gentleman's Magazine, 102.
Geographical distribution, 26.
Gerard, 138.
Gibbon, 113.
Gilpin, 5, 113.
Giraldus Cambrensis, 96.
Gisborne, 167.
Glamis Castle, 92.
Glasnevin, 18.
Glencormack, 16, 94.
Glendalough, 44.
Glenmoriston, 92.
Gormanstown, 17.
Goytre, 49, 86, 95.
Grange-Con, 20.
Gravetye, 89.
Gray, 169.
Gresford, 50, 82, 217.
Grognier, Professor, 140.
Guildsfield, 218.
Gyffin, 82.

HADDON, 12.
Hadham, 9.
Hambledon, Hants, 83.
Hambledon, Surrey, 49, 87, 95, 218.
Hampstead-Marshall, 81, 95.
Hansard, 104.
Hardham, Hants, 83.
Hardham, Sussex, 88, 219.

Harlington, 11, 85, 220.
Harrietsham, 85, 95.
Harrow School, 130.
Hartbourne Tarrant, 52.
Hartburn, 86.
Harte, 167.
Hartig and Weber, 69.
Hatton House, 92.
Haworth Castle, 82.
Hayes, 17, 34, 44.
Headfort, 11.
Hedsor, 81.
Heer, Professor, 29.
Helmarton Lodge, 12.
Henbury, 9, 83, 221.
Henry IV., Commission, 104.
Henry VIII., Act of, 124.
Herbert, Lord, 123.
Herrick, 165.
Heslington, 11.
Heywood, 163.
Hinley Hall, 87.
Hollow trees becoming solid, 80.
Homer, 154.
Hood, 170.
Hooker, Sir Joseph, 27, 158.
Hurdlestone, 18.
Hurstmonceaux, 89, 95, 222.
Hutchison, 62.
Hutton, John, 12.

ICKLESHAM, 49, 89.
Iffley, 49, 86, 223.
Inchbald, 71.
Inch Lonaig, 31, 41, 80, 91, 224.
Irish trees of 10 feet in girth, 93.

JAMES, CAPTAIN, 33.

KEATS, 171.
Kidbroke, 84.
Killesleigh Castle, 93.
Kilmacannac, 94.
Kilteevon, 18.
Kinglye Vale, 20, 60, 89.
Kinlet, 86.
Kirton of Forgan, 92.

Knight, 8.
Kyre Park, 49, 80, 89, 90, 95, 225.

LAMBERHURST, 85.
Lanercost, 82.
Lateran Council, decree of, 134.
Latimer, Bishop, 122.
Lavant, East, 89.
Lawen, 92.
Leeds (Kent), 85, 95, 227.
Leges Wallicæ, 110.
Leigh Court, 87.
Levens, 11.
Leyden, 169.
Lightfoot, Bishop, 114.
Lindfield, 88.
Llanbedrog, 76.
Llandegai, 82.
Llandegri, 14.
Llanfoist, 86, 95.
Llangeitho, 81.
Llanlellyd, 85.
Llanthewy Bach, 80, 85, 95, 227.
Longleat, 89.
Long Sutton, 83.
Lorton, 89, 228.
Loudon, 109, 132, 150.
Loudon Castle, 91.
Lough Corrib, 231.
Loughcrew, 93.
Lucan, 157.

MACKINTOSH, SIR JAMES, 169.
Madden, 27.
Maeslaugh Castle, 86.
Magna Charta, 102.
Mamhilad, 80, 85, 95, 233.
Manaton, 82.
Mant, Bishop, 170.
Manwood, 119.
Maynooth, 76, 93.
Medmenham, 81.
Melbourne, 12, 14.
Melksham Court, 234.
Meyrick, 118.
Mickleham Downs, 87.

Milford, 9, 11, 94.
Moira, 93.
Mount Wilson, 16.
Muckross Abbey, 93, 235.
Munro, Professor, 146, 148.

NETHER PLACE, 77.
Newland's Corner, 32.
Newth, 139.
Norbury Park, 78, 88, 236.
Norman bow, 112.
Norman cross-bow, 132.
Northiam, 12, 49, 85, 236.
Northington, 83.
Notable trees of 10' feet in girth, 81.

O'BRIEN, CAPTAIN, 109.
Old Castle, 92.
Old Meldrum Manse, 51, 91.
Ormiston Hall, 63, 92, 240.
Ossian, 96.
Overcrowding, effects of, 69.
Overton, 83.
Overton-on-Dee, 14.

PACKWOOD, 7.
Painswick, 14.
Palgrave, Mr. F. T., 159.
Palms, 99.
Pant Cllydw, 76, 81, 95.
Parkhill, 52, 92.
Parkinson, 139.
Parnell, 165.
Patterdale, 89, 242.
Penrhyn Park, 82.
Percival, Dr., 142.
Peterchurch, 84.
Petham, 84.
Pewsey, 14.
Philip and Mary, Statute of, 124.
Philip de Comines, 115.
Pitmedden, 52, 60, 91.
Pliny, 137, 156, 158.
Plutarch, 136.
Poictiers, 115.
Pollarding, effect of, 66.

Index

Pope, 6.
Portbury, 67, 80, 87, 242.
Prior, 167.
Puckington, 49, 86, 243.

RAGLAN, 85.
Ramsay, 20.
Rate of growth in young trees, 55.
Rate of growth in old trees, 61.
Rathkenny House, 94.
Reynal, 143.
Ribbesford, 244.
Richard II., Act of, 115, 120.
Richard III., 103, 121.
Robinson, Mr. W., 4, 8, 27.
Rockingham, 10, 12.
Rockmanshull House, 94.
Roebuck Castle, 20.
Rogers, 175.
Rokeby, 67.
Roseneath, 14, 48, 91, 245.
Rossanagh, 18, 94.
Rossdhu, 91.
Rossfad, 93.
Rosslyn, 92.
Royal Company of Archers, 127.
Ruskin, 112, 172, 174.

ST. JOHN IN THE WILDERNESS, 82.
Saint's Yew, 110.
Sanderstead, 48, 87, 245.
Schowle, 83, 95.
Schroff, 145.
Scott, Sir W., 114, 171.
Scottish superstition, 105.
Scottish yews of 10 feet in girth, 91.
Selborne, 83.
Selby, 139.
Shakespeare, 163.
Shelley, 173.
Shirley, 166.
Shorne, 74, 89, 247.
Shortgrove, 82.
Shotterel and Darfey, 168.
Slane, 94.
South Hayling, 84, 95.

Speldhurst, 84, 249.
Spenser, 159, 160.
Spotborough Hall, 90.
Squarey, 146.
Stanley, Thomas, 99.
Stanstead, 80, 84, 249.
Stanton, 89.
Statius, 98, 137.
Stedham, 89.
Steep, 84.
Stoke Courcy, 49, 86.
Stoke Gabriel, 49, 82.
Stokestown Ho., 94.
Stow, 129.
Stowting, 49, 85.
Strutt, 105.
Stuart-Wortley, 143.
Studley Park, 89.
Swift, 168.
Synonyms, 22.

TANDRIDGE, 87, 95, 250.
Taylor, Professor, 139.
Tardebigge, 96.
Taxin, 152.
Taxin, a cardiac tonic, 146.
Taxus adpressa, 21.
T. aurea, 21.
T. baccata, 19.
T. baccata fastigiata, 20.
Tegetmeier, 152.
Tennyson, Lord, 163, 175.
Tettenhall, 87.
Theophrastus, 138.
Thompson, Dr., 140.
Thoresby, 34.
Thurnham, 84.
Tintern, 28, 85, 250.
Tisbury, 49, 89, 95, 251.
Titsey Place, 88.
Traditional accounts, 58.
Trentham, 49, 87, 95, 252.
Tudesley, 84.
Tytherley, 50, 55, 89, 254.

ULCOMBE, 84, 95, 255.

VALUE OF YEW IN WALES, 109.
Varieties of Taxus, 20.
Veitch, Mr., 20.
'Vew,' 'View,' 24.
Virgil, 137, 155.

WARBLINGTON, 83, 95.
Ward, Mrs. Humphry, 13.
Warlingham, 87.
Watcombe, 81, 86, 256.
Wellow, 55.
Westbury-on-Trim, 83, 248.
Westfelton, 257.
Whittinghame, 92, 257.
Why planted in churchyards, 96.
Wiborg, Professor, 150.
Wilton House, 258.
Wilmington, 89.
Windlesham, 87.
Windsor Forest, 258.
Winterbourne, 51, 56.

Withering, 29.
Withycombe, 82, 95.
Wood, characters and uses of, 107.
Wood, rings of, 77.
Woodmen of Arden, 127.
Woolbeding, 88.
Wordsworth, 173.
Wolton, 87.
Wrest, 12.

YATTENDEN, 48, 49, 81, 259.
Yester, 92.
Yewdale, 89.
Yew-trees of 10 feet in girth in England, 81.
Yew-trees of 10 feet in girth in Ireland, 93.
Yew-trees of 10 feet in girth in Scotland, 91.
Yew-trees of 30 feet in girth in England, 95.

Printed by T. and A. CONSTABLE, Printers to Her Majesty
at the Edinburgh University Press

www.ingramcontent.com/pod-product-compliance
Lightning Source LLC
Chambersburg PA
CBHW030739230426
43667CB00007B/771